FOUR CAUSES OF REALITY

FOUR CAUSES OF REALITY

by WILLIAM CREWS

PHILOSOPHICAL LIBRARY
New York

CONTENTS

I. INTRODUCTION 1

Four View Points 2
World Picture of the Four Causes 5
Entity 7
The Formal Explanation of Reality Through
    Metaphysics 8
The Concept of Entity 8
Difference Between Entity and Being 9
Entity and the Material Cause 10
The Material Cause and a Given Realm of Reality 11
Material 12
Material and the Thinker 13
Confusion of Terms 15
Location of Prime Matter 16
Matter 18
Form 19
Motion: The Third Major Ingredient for a Becoming .. 19
Basic Difference Between This Demonstration
    and Aristotle 22
Priority of Matter ... Then Form ... Then Motion ... 24
The Eternal Trinity for Anything 25
First Cause Only Concerned with the Necessary
    Potential 25
Four Ways in Which Entity Is Considered 26
Chain Reaction of the Three Major Ingredients 27
Entity the Material Cause 28
Matter, Form and Motion All Considered
    Material in Entity 29

CONTENTS (continued)

All Things Are Considered as Form in the
Second Cause 30
All Things Are Considered in Terms of Fruition in
the Third Cause 30
The Fourth Cause Is Only Concerned with the
Final Purpose 31
Summation of the Causes 32
Materiality Stressed by the Early Greek Thinkers 33
Entity Is Potential, Not Actual 35
Entity the Start 37
Eternity of the Trinity 38
Reality for Aristotle 39
Bare Bones of the First Cause 41

II. THE SECOND PRESENTATION OF
REALITY 42

Three Parts to the Development of Beings
Which We Experience 43
The Four Causes Presented in the Second Cause 43
Actuality Is the Opposite of Potential 44
Actual Being 44
Specific Being 45
The Individual Being 46
Existence 47
The Categories 50
Second Three Categories 51
Operation 54

III. THE THIRD PRESENTATION OF REALITY:
THE FRUITION OF THINGS 57

Fruition Related to Motion 59
Values and Fruitfulness 61
The Value of Fullness 64
Personalization 67
Parts of a Personality 67
Summation of the Third Cause 71

CONTENTS (continued)

IV. THE FOURTH PRESENTATION OF REALITY 73

The Term Oneness 75
Oneness in the Fourth Cause 76
Third Goal of the Fourth Cause 78
Wholeness of the Becoming 79
Wholeness in the Second Cause 80
Wholeness in the Third Cause 80
Wholeness in the Fourth Cause 81
Summation of the Fourth Cause 81
The Four Causes Covered Intellectually 82
Causes in History 83
The First Cause: the Becoming, the Overall Picture .. 84
The Second Cause: the Being, the Overall Picture 85
The End of the Second Cause: the Overall Picture 86
The Third Cause: the Overall Picture 88
The Fourth Cause: the Overall Picture 88
Polarization of the Four Causes 89
A Specific Picture of the Working of the
    Four Causes 91
Greek History and the Four Causes 93
Jewish History and the Four Causes 94
The Four Causes in Our Individual Society 96
First Period of Our Civilization 96
Our Civilization Devoted to the Fruition of Mankind .. 97
Church History a Good Guide to the Working
    of the Causes 98
Four Causes Expressing Themselves in Political Life .. 99
The Second Period in Our Society 100
Scholasticism: The Intellectual Development 101
The Third Cause in Our Society 102
The Fourth Cause in Our History 105
Dominant Personalities 106
The Four Causes and Religion 109
Martin Luther and the Third Cause 110
Natural Conflict Between Second and Third Cause 112

CONTENTS (continued)

Conflict Seems to Be Always Present Between
the Causes 114
Four Causes and the Individual Thing 117
Four Causes in the Bible 118
Summing up The Four Causes in History 120
The Causes and the Rest of the World 126
The Third Cause and the United States 128
Moving Along 132
Chinese Personality 133
Whole World Offers Four Views of Reality 136
Governments: Schools: Christianity 136
Chinese and the Fourth Cause 139
Four Points of the Compass 140
The Conception of the Supreme Being According
to the Four Causes 141

Definitions 145
First Cause 150
Second Cause 151
Third Cause 152
Fourth Cause 153

Epilogue 155

I. INTRODUCTION

Why study causes? Because the understanding of causes will enable us to gain a fuller comprehension of the reality we experience. Cause gives us a reference point in which to view reality. Without this reference point no ultimate judgment can be possible concerning the reality of our experience; and no coherent and consistent understanding of reality can be achieved without this reference point.

There have been many men who have undertaken the examination of causes, so this work has no claim to being a pioneer study. What I hope to accomplish is a fuller and deeper understanding of causes, thereby adding something new to our knowledge of reality. I hope to show in this work how one's point of view determines the view of the whole of reality; and how, by understanding our view and the view of other people, a total comprehension of the whole of reality can be accomplished.

I would like to demonstrate the four basic ways in which mankind views reality. These four views are not only mental views but also geological as well as historical, and are based upon the four causes. We all need a starting point and a guide in which to view things. We need a tool in which to pry open our minds to total reality. This tool consists of the four causes. We all need a picture window to look out upon the world. No person or society is capable of viewing reality from a vacuum. The society of the United States has a world view in which the individual, his rights and his pursuit of happiness are considered to be the ultimate goal. This is a valid viewpoint but it is not necessarily the only one. We shall see that there are three other valid goals that a given society may strive to fulfill. We need not give up our own personal or social viewpoint, but having an understanding of the other three views will relieve our confusion and misunderstanding of other societies and will give us an understanding of the whole.

FOUR VIEW POINTS

Reality, and by reality is meant the whole of experience that we feel and understand, is governed by four causes. These four causes each produce an effect, and the sum total of these effects produces a cycle. Each cause contributes one-fourth to the full cycle. A complete understanding of the four causes will allow an understanding of the complete cycle of reality. The four causes follow in succession: the causes are called the first cause, the second cause, the third cause and the fourth cause. They can also be called the beginning cause, the formal cause, the efficient cause and the final cause. They can also be called the *entity* cause, the *being* cause, the *fruitional* cause, and the *realized* cause. Each cause can be called various names depending upon our conception of it, but regardless of names, each cause has a specific and definite job to perform in the presentation of reality. This is the purpose of the causes—the presentation of reality, or the presentation of an effect. A cause is that thing which produces an effect, and this effect or this product is called reality. The causes we will be interested in are only those causes which are needed to bring about reality, any reality.

These causes produce the reoccurrence of similar happenings. We all perceive that there is a pattern repeating itself in the world, and this we call the cycle in history. As new things come into reality we unconsciously perceive that these things fit into a pattern that has repeated itself many times over. We say that this pattern is the foundation of our concept of the "law of nature" or the "rule of nature." In order to have some connection with the past, with the present and with the future, there must be some pattern. This is how all reality is fused together, for regardless of who, what, or which the thing is, having all things progress through a similar pattern produces a communication of similar existences in reality. This results in *one* reality. The becoming, the being, the fruition and the finalization of a thing are the phases which any and all things undergo in this reality. This pattern results in the total presentation of this particular reality, which also means that we all live life from the same book.

It has been said in our age (because we are going through a period of change or transition) that all things are relative. There is truth to this axiom, but it is not the whole truth. Any and all things relate to certain definite and precise causes. These causes are very definite and must be so in order to produce reality. What brings about the change we are experiencing in our history and in our age is the transition from one cause to another. We are living in an age in which one cause is phasing itself out and a new cause is taking its place in history. One part of human society will content itself to look at reality from the phase that produced the present reality, while another segment of the society will seek to bring forth the next phase. A conflict of interests arises and the older generation loses contact with the younger. The child views reality from the becoming or the material cause. When he becomes older and able to start forming himself, he views reality from the formative cause which concentrated upon the development of his identity and the operation of his being. Later, as he becomes more mature, he starts to produce things and he becomes more attentive to the fruitional or efficient cause. Finally, as he grows older, he becomes more attentive to the realization or the purpose of the reality. Naturally, the mature person is not attentive to the becoming of things, nor is the youth interested in the production of things. This is the way in which things are relative to the viewpoint in which a person views reality.

This also applies to the history of a people, a nation or a civilization. In the becoming stage of the society, the viewpoint of the society will be different from that of the formative period. Society will view the productive period differently than the formative years, and during the period in which society is realizing itself, its view then will be different than the other three views which at one time held its interest. Things are relative, but all things relate to one of the four basic and ultimate causes. These causes, as we shall see, are absolute and must be eternal in order for any reality to be present.

If we look at all the created reality, the whole visible universe with all its galaxies, all the billions of stars, all the millions of planets and all the star clusters, each and every one of these things goes through four phases of reality. We can speak of the four causes as they relate to the whole of the visible universe, or as they relate to the one particular world as we experience it, to our society and to us as individuals. These four causes will also be related to the unseen reality of which we know so little. Regardless of what reality we are referring to and regardless of what thing in this reality is specified, there will always be these four causes, which must account for the reality. It is these causes which allow us to have a full understanding of both the seen and the unseen reality, and this is why they are considered to be of value for men to understand.

We live in one segment of world society. This generally is called the Western Civilization. Naturally, this segment of society will emphasize one phase of the total world cycle. Other world views will not be here given the full study or thought that the one in which we live will be given. The West at one time in the past has emphasized the first or the becoming cause. This was during the period of the "becoming to be" of Western European society. This period spanned the so-called Dark Ages and lasted for about 500 years. Next came the formative period, which lasted from 1000 A.D. to 1500 A.D. This was the period of the Middle Ages, in which the formation of all the institutions of our civilization came into development. Next is the period in which we are living, and this is the fruitional phase. This is the period in which the production of things is considered to be of the greatest importance, and this period has the same life span: 500 years. The period is now approaching an end, and the beginning of the final period is taking place. This next period will be concerned with the realization of our civilization and with the finalization and the completion of our civilization, and after the realization has been completed the cycle will begin again (if the world is still here). The last period has the same span of time in which to develop as the other three periods, which is 500 years.

WORLD PICTURE OF THE FOUR CAUSES

We shall see that the primitive or the pre-historic people viewed reality from the window of the first cause. The historical period, culminating with the union of the Romans, Greeks and Jews, was the full development of the formal period of human civilization. Western Civilization has emphasized the third cause, the production of human society or the fruition of human civilization. The best example of the final cause has been portrayed by the Chinese. Their emphasis upon the practical and the final purposes of this reality has been their main concern since the beginning of the Chinese society.

It can be and will be seen that the emphasis of a particular cause is relative to certain groups of people in different parts of the world. The age of the society will emphasize a certain cause at one period and neglect other causes during that same period.

The child lives in the context of the first cause or the becoming. The youth lives in that of the second cause, or the formation of being. The mature person is concerned with his fruition and the products that he produces in the reality. The aged person is concerned with the fourth cause, the realization of his reality and the harmonization of this reality with the whole of reality.

In order not to confuse a difficult subject, the best thing to do is to understand each cause in itself and how it is related to the other causes without referring to any particular thing or to any particular reality. When we do this we

5

move into the field of metaphysics, where the point of interest is the various causes in themselves, with no dependence upon any particular realm of reality. This is what the concept of metaphysics is all about, it is concerned with the causes beyond the realm of any particular level of reality.

We will then be talking about the four positive causes which contribute to the full presentation of reality. But we must also take into consideration the four negative sides of these causes, which are as follows:

1. The first cause is the first positive side or the first presentation of reality; the negative side of this is nonreality. The first cause presents a possibility for reality; the negative side of this, or the contrary, is non-reality.

2. The second cause presents the positive actual formation of the thing or being; the negative, or the contrary, is the non-being of reality. Notice it is not the non-reality but the non-being of reality.

3. The third cause presents the fruition of reality; the negative, or the contrary, is the frustration of reality or the non-productiveness or barrenness of reality.

4. Finally, the fourth cause presents the purpose and the full realization of reality; the contrary is the negative disharmony which is the result of a lack of complete finalization of the reality.

We mention the positive as well as the negative for the one can not be without the other. Each cause offers something positive and necessary for the full presentation of reality, and when the full positive presentation is lacking the negative or contrary side of the cause dominates. It is necessary to keep the two sides of any cause in mind when considering the effects of the cause.

The first positive presentation of the first cause is that which is opposite non-reality, and the *universal* effect of the first cause is *entity*. Entity is the universal positive presentation of the first cause. Entity is opposite to universal concept of non-reality, so let us see what the positive universal concept of *entity* is all about.

ENTITY

Most people believe that something is necessary to support the experienced reality in which we have our existence. Many people say that the cause that supports our experienced reality is "one ultimate cause" called the Supreme Being or the ultimate creator or some other deity referred to as the one ultimate and absolute cause of this reality. Other persons may take the negative side and say that the causes that support our observed reality consist ultimately of demons. This need to explain the ultimate cause supporting reality is a common psychological need of all peoples at all times. This idea and this need—that something is necessary to support the reality of our experience— is expressed in all the religious beliefs throughout mankind. The Greeks completed for the ancient world the intellectual explanation of the causes which were thought to be needed in order to support anything. The beginning of Greek thought concerned itself with the concept of matter or material as the first necessary ingredient needed in order for anything to exist. It is the contention of this work that the most important first ingredient needed in order for any thing to exist is the material. It is also the contention that this is what the concept of *entity* is all about—*material*.

Entity is the first universal presentation of reality; this also means that the first universal presentation of reality will be all about matter or material. Material and entity to this writer mean the same thing. Entity in the most universal concept, or material in the same way, will not be found in this or in any other reality but in the science of metaphysics. This science does not concern itself with any particular realm of reality or any particular physical being. What it does concern itself with are the major requirements needed so that there can be a universal concept of

7

Entity. The most universal of concepts will be found in the science of Metaphysics; consequently this science will embrace all realms and all regions of reality: that which we experience and that which we are not capable of experiencing, the seen as well as the unseen, the touched as well as the untouched.

THE FORMAL EXPLANATION OF REALITY THROUGH METAPHYSICS

Metaphysics attempts to explain in a formal and rational manner what is needed to support reality. No consideration is given to positive or negative religious belief. What this science historically has done is to demonstrate in a formal way what is required to have reality, any kind of reality. To accomplish this purpose the concept of Entity has been used from the very start of this method of philosophy as the starting point of its demonstration.

THE CONCEPT OF ENTITY

The concept of Entity is as old as philosophy, and it is through Aristotle that we know that the ancients of Greece formulated and used it in their demonstrations. Aristotle began his philosophy with the concept of Entity, and although he did not make, as we shall show, all the major distinctions necessary to fully explain the becoming or the beginning of reality, he should be given full credit for starting with the proper concept. There are a great number of people who think that the concept of Entity and the concept of Being are one and the same thing but only used in different ways. This is where many, many errors start. The concept of Entity refers to only one cause and one cause alone, and that is the first cause. The concept of Being refers only to the second cause and not to the first, third or fourth. Each concept has a definite place and a definite cause to which it refers, and the concepts are not interchangeable.

8

Entity refers to the first cause and it is concerned with the *universal* concept of *becoming*. Further on we shall see what is involved in becoming, but the universal understanding of becoming is Entity. The universal idea of becoming deals with the concept as it can be applied to any and all things and in any and all realities. Nothing is exempt, for all things have a becoming. To most people becoming refers to a development of something that is already present; however, this idea is limited and does not apply to the universal idea of becoming. In the universal idea of becoming, no period of development is referred to and no particular thing is referred to. The only concern in the universal idea of becoming is the necessary major ingredients needed to produce a becoming. Nothing is established in a becoming, nothing is identified and nothing is operating. This concept is only concerned with supplying the necessary major ingredients so that there can be a general possibility of some specific thing becoming an individual. Entity is then concerned only with the necessary major requirements, so that there can be some possibility of reality becoming. Next to Entity is non-reality, or the non-possibility of any becoming.

Nowhere in the universal concept of Entity is there Being. Being has nothing to do with the concept of Entity; however, Entity provides through its universal concept of becoming the foundation for Being.

Being is the universal concept referring to something definite and established. The universal concept of Being is concerned with some "kind of" thing, a thing that has established itself as some definite *one* thing, a thing that has an identity and a thing that has some type of operation. Being qua Being is concerned with the major *principles* that determine the oneness of a Being, that determine the identity of a Being and that determine the operation of any and all Beings.

Being is founded upon the second cause and it is the

universal concept providing for the major principles which determine any and all beings. The general concept of Being is *actuality* and the specific demonstration of Being is *substance*, while the individual demonstration of Being is through the essence, existence and operation of the Being.

Entity has the ability of being neuter. It does not entail the question of "kind of" or determination. Entity deals with a whole set of problems that Being knows nothing about. Being is not concerned with providing the major ingredients necessary to becoming. Being is only concerned with providing the major *principles* to establish determination. A becoming is the first presentation of reality and Entity is concerned with the universal presentation of becoming.

ENTITY AND THE MATERIAL CAUSE

Entity represents the material cause in the broadest terms, which is the universal principle applying to any and all things. Entity refers to the universal need for any and all things to have material as the first function of reality. The universal material needed for any becoming is matter, form and motion. We shall discuss these three major ingredients later in this chapter. The general understanding of the first cause is that it offers the substrata for some reality. Last, but not the least, is the individual understanding of the first cause which concerns the individual becoming of matter, form and motion.

It can be seen that the material cause is a larger concept than Entity. Entity is only concerned with the universal manifestation of the first cause. However, contained in the universal is also the general, the specific and the individual manifestations of the first cause. We can say that the Entity for any and all things will posess the potential, the specific and the individual major ingredients needed for becoming. If we wish to speak about the Entity of a Supreme Being, the same will apply to the Entity of a man or a duck or a deer. Every material cause and every becoming posesses the universal, the general, the specific and the individual.

THE MATERIAL CAUSE AND A GIVEN
REALM OF REALITY

Applying the first cause to the realm of reality in which the Creator of all things is said to reside will be no different than applying the first cause to the reality of man. A creator is something and not nothing, and the most universal manifestation of a creator is the supreme Entity. This represents the supreme becoming of a reality that is other than non-reality. The general manifestation of this supreme reality is that it offers a definite potential. The specific manifestation of the first cause is that a substratum is present in which a definite foundation is determined. The individual determination of this first cause offering a becoming is the definite presentation of matter, form and motion allowing an individual becoming to take place.

Applying the first cause to the reality of man follows the same pattern and deals with the same concepts. The only difference will be the "kind of" material and the realm of reality that applies. The realm of reality that applies to a supreme creator will be different from the reality that is a part of its creation through the material that makes up each entity. The universal becoming of a creator concerns itself with a definite material and so does the universal becoming of a man. Each material is different from the other but it is material all the same. The becoming of a man offers a general potentiality for a given realm of reality. A becoming offers a foundation for a specific kind of being that will eventually occur. A becoming offers the possibility for some individual thing when there is a becoming of a certain definite kind of matter, form and motion. The major material ingredients for the supreme creator are matter, form and motion. The major material ingredients for the becoming of a man are matter, form and motion. The same major ingredients are necessary for any given realm of reality but what makes literally all the difference in the world is the kind of material that is involved in the becoming.

MATERIAL

The only thing that is determined in the first cause is the necessity for having material begin the process of presenting reality. In the first cause the becoming revolves around the material that is presented. Each cause, as we shall see, determines something in the reality. This is the effect that it produces and this is why it is called a cause. What the first cause determines is the material. The second cause will determine the formation of the being; the third cause will determine the fruition; the fourth cause will determine the finalization of the reality.

Materiality determines in which realm of reality a becoming is to take place, or where the first presentation of a reality is to be presented. The materiality of a supreme being is different from the materiality of an angel or the materiality of a man. So, depending upon the material, a becoming will take place in one realm of reality and not in another. Thus the material makes all the difference. Material determines what realm of reality one is to have a becoming in; it also determines the general, the specific and the individual becoming. The material becoming of a duck is different from that of a man. The only thing that the first cause is concerned with is to determine the possibility of some becoming in a given realm of reality.

The material offers the becoming, but the state of becoming is not concerned with the fully formed or developed thing. When something is fully developed and formed, then the second cause must be consulted, for this is the effect of the second cause and not the effect of the first cause. Of all the causes the first is the most important, for without the first cause there can't be any possibility of anything to follow. The other three causes depend upon the first cause to present the opportunity for all that is to follow. But because the first cause does not concern itself with a determined and identified thing, it is often overlooked in importance and given little attention. The result is that most thinkers start with the second cause or the Being of reality

12

and the result is that they simply have no foundation under their work. It is the first cause which supports all that is to follow. To think that the determination of the material is not important is to literally make the greatest mistake possible. This has been done down through the ages and will continue on down through the ages when little or no consideration is given to the first cause. How many times has it been mentioned that man lives in a material world and that the angels and the supreme being live in worlds that are called non-material or spiritual? It is certainly proper to distinguish one realm of reality from another, but it is not correct to think that only man's reality contains material. Man's reality contains a "certain kind of" material which is different from the material of the angels and the material of the supreme creator. That is why material makes all the difference between living in one reality or living in another reality. The material determines in what realm of reality becoming will take place.

MATERIAL AND THE THINKER

The intellectual, the rational man and the thinker are all inclined to pass over the concept of materiality very quickly. These people deal with ideas and concepts which appear in many cases to be divorced from material. They are inclined to conclude that the ultimate reduction of all things does not contain any material. Thus an Aristotle will say that the ultimate reduction of all things is the form. According to Aristotle and the other thinkers who follow his viewpoint, it will be the form that is the supporting foundation of reality. This idea provokes all kinds of problems because of the wrong starting point. When form is said to be the first thing presented in reality there is no room for becoming, and the result is that one is likely to hear of such thing as spontaneous generation or unmoved mover or instant beings. These terms arise because there is no foundation supporting being. The result of all this is that the supreme being is thought of as "the perfect form."

13

The angels are thought of as each comprising a single specie, their reality being modeled after the "perfect ideas" in the mind of the creator. This may be a nice way of explaining reality to a child, but it doesn't hold much water to a person who gives a little thought to the matter.

Why there has been an aversion to matter or to the material can perhaps be explained by history better than by anything else. We know that there has been and there continues to be some contention between governments, schools and churches. The result of this has been the emphasis that each of the contenders places upon their particular view of reality. Governments place all their emphasis upon the material, the land and the amount of people and the resources at their disposal. Schools emphasize the intellectual, the literary and the cultural accomplishments of their students in grasping the ideas that are presented. Churches emphasize the moral and the spiritual side of man. Each domain carefully refrains from infringing upon the domain of the other. The result is that a society that is concerned with the distribution of the goods of this world is called materialist. The schools, which are concerned only with ideas, are called ivory towers and idealistic. And the churches are called pies-in-the-sky or sky-writers. When the church people speak they speak of the supreme being as something spiritual; when the intellectuals speak of the supreme being he is something that revolves around a perfect form; and when the government speaks of the supreme being he is the ultimate provider. These are the historical reasons why the idea of materiality as being the foundation of all things has not been readily accepted by the majority of the people in Western Civilization. There has been a continuing distrust between the three contenders for reality, and the result has been as expected: each places its emphasis upon that realm of reality that concerns them and leaves the rest to silence.

This is a work in constructive philosophy and it is its intention to join hands with everyone and to show where each cause has its place in the scheme of things. Placing

14

materiality in the first order of importance takes into consideration the necessity of material as the first order of importance; this in turn gives rise to the need for the formation of things and the need for a second cause which is concerned with the formal ordering of reality; this in turn gives rise to the need for the individuation of reality which is the province of the third cause.

CONFUSION OF TERMS

The biggest problem in the understanding of the first cause has been the inability of thinkers to give a precise definition to all the terms that are found in the first cause. There has always been some confusion between the terms "material" and "matter." In the explanation given of the first cause, everything in the cause is some kind of material by the very nature of its belonging to the first cause, but everything in the first cause is not matter. Matter is just one major ingredient among two other equally important ingredients. The ultimate effect of the first cause is to determine in which reality a becoming takes place. The first cause is thus concerned with the determination of the becoming reality in all its aspects. Not only is it concerned with what realm of reality the becoming is to take place in but also with the becoming itself, for it is concerned with supplying the three major ingredients needed so that a becoming can happen. Aristotle among others confused matter with material and then went on to say that matter implies indeterminateness and thus can not be admitted in a primary way in the Entity.

Each cause must produce some effect and to have indeterminateness in the first cause would be contrary to all reason, for this is a negative side effect and does not offer a positive contribution to the explanation of reality. However, Aristotle was not able to see what positive contribution to reality material does make; consequently form had to take the first place in the order of priority in the explanation of reality. This was Aristotle's biggest mistake, for it

15

was similar to putting the cart before the horse. Formation or development can not take place without some material in which to develop and this was what Aristotle ultimately concluded. For him the form had to be the ultimate first cause, for it was responsible for being the cause which produced the full development of the thing. There is no denying that form does produce the full development of the thing; but it does not produce a becoming and it is necessary to have becoming before there can be Being. This is what the material cause is all about, the production of becoming which revolves around three major material ingredients called matter, form and motion. If the material cause is fully understood, nobody can have any objection to placing the material cause in the first order of priority and the formal cause in the second order. Each cause produces its own effect which complements the other cause and is not in any way contrary to the other. Since Aristotle was not able to see the positive effect of the first cause, he placed the second cause in place of the first. The result was his emphasis upon the formal development of Being and not upon the first development, which is Becoming.

LOCATION OF PRIME MATTER

Even stressing form as the ultimate reduction of all things still does not relieve the contradiction, from reality itself, that material must come first. For this reason it was necessary to invent Prime Matter. First of all there is no such thing as Prime Matter. However, there is such a thing as Prime Material. Prime Material consists of the three major primary ingredients needed to allow becoming to take place. The primary material ingredients are matter, form and motion. For becoming to take place, a certain kind of matter is necessary; this can be called the prime matter of the particular becoming. The matter needed to make a house or a man is of a definite kind, and each matter is called prime to that particular becoming. There is no overall prime matter which can be applied to this realm of

16

reality and to all other realms of reality. Matter is the determining ingredient; matter determines whether the being will be in the realm of the creator, in the realm of the angels or in the realm of man's experience. But there is such a thing as Prime Material, and this refers to the primary material ingredients needed in order for anything to become. As we have said, these material ingredients are matter, form and motion. These primary material ingredients *do* apply to any and all things in this or any other reality.

To the reality of the creator, to the reality of the angels, to the reality of man—any reality whatsoever—there must be three primary material ingredients present. These ingredients are called the *prime material*. It is this confusion between material and matter that has caused so much perplexity on the part of thinkers. Material ingredients apply to things separated and distinct from each other. Thus, to make a house, certain kinds of building matter is needed, a certain kind of plan is needed, and the motion of the skilled tradesmen is required: all three things are the prime material ingredients necessary for the becoming of a house. The matter that makes a house is different from the matter that makes a living thing such as a man. Water is the common matter for all living things; blood is the determining form of the species, and the spirit is the motion which allows a becoming of a man to occur.

If one limits his description of things and refers only to a certain specific area of reality such as the living things on earth, then one can say that the prime matter of all living things on earth is water. Water is the prime matter of all living things on earth. That is about as far as one can go with prime matter. One cannot say anything about totality for this entire realm of reality, because the term does not extend that far. It extends only as far as a general becoming. We say that water is necessary for all living things and this water can be called the prime matter of all living things but not prime for all things. Prime material extends to any and all things seen and unseen, experienced

17

and not experienced. There is quite a difference between the two terms, and when this is not distinguished from the very beginning confusion will result. Prime material refers to any and all becomings, regardless of where they take place or in what realm of reality. Prime matter does refer to some definite kind of becoming and to a definite realm of reality. This must be understood from the very beginning.

MATTER

The term matter is laced with difficulties only if one loses grasp of the definitions and the part that each ingredient plays in the becoming of things. Matter is one of the three major ingredients needed so that a becoming can take place. Matter is the first major ingredient, and it provides the possibility for a becoming to take place in a given realm of reality. Matter determines in what realm there will occur a new becoming. Matter is the first necessary ingredient for an individual becoming. In the case of living things, the matter will be water, which is the first necessity for an individual becoming. Water is the basic matter applying to all living things; thus, it can be called the *prime matter* for all living things on earth . . . but not the prime material. Some kind of matter is common to a general class of things and only in this can we call matter the prime matter. All the matter that is used in building houses can be called prime matter for houses, but not for anything else. So, prime matter is only that matter which is necessary for a general class of things, but matter, any kind of matter, is the first material ingredient necessary for becoming. Matter determines the realm of reality that a becoming will take place in and it determines the general classification of the becoming. The matter that provides for a house determines that it is in a non-living classification, while the matter (water) for a man determines the becoming to be in a living classification. Those people who think that a supreme being or an angel are without matter are sadly mistaken in their conception of things, for it is indeed matter that determines whether a being is a man or an angel or a supreme being.

FORM

The second material ingredient necessary for a becoming is the material ingredient which determines the species or specifies what class the becoming is to take place in. Form is a material ingredient composed of some kind of matter. It is impossible to think of anything that is not composed of matter in one way or another and form is no exception. The form or the design determines what specific becoming is to take place in the general reality which was determined by the matter. We have seen that water supplies the common matter for any and all living things in our realm of reality. Blood is the form which determines what a specific thing will become. Whether the becoming thing will be a dog, cat, horse, bird or man will depend upon its blood, which specifies the kind of becoming that will take place. The matter used to build houses supplies the general possibility for the becoming of a building; the plans specify what kind of house it will become. Form by itself is never separated from matter for if, in the example of a house, the design is either drawn on paper or is in the mind of the designer: in either place, matter is necessary to support the form. When a becoming is taking place, the design is specifying itself in the given general matter, allowing a specific kind of becoming to take place; at no instance is matter missing from the becoming.

MOTION: THE THIRD MAJOR INGREDIENT FOR A BECOMING

So far we have considered two major ingredients which supply a definite need so that a becoming can take place; the matter supplies the general possibility for a becoming and the form supplies the specific possibility for a becoming. To complete a becoming a third major material ingredient is needed. This ingredient is motion.

In the example of the house, we have seen that matter offers the common building materials which allow for a general becoming of a house. We have seen also that the plans or the design allow for the becoming of a certain kind of house. Now, unless motion is introduced there can be no finalization of the becoming, there can be no individual house. In our example, the motion would be the skilled movement of the tradesmen who translate the design and the common matter into a specific house. The movement or work of the tradesmen allow for an individual becoming to take place and this completes the ingredients necessary for a becoming to take place. In the case of a man, the motion is the spirit or the soul which individuates the person and allows for the individual to be possible. This spirit is dependent upon the common matter of water and the specific material of blood for the possibility of an individual person becoming. We see, therefore, the necessity of having three major ingredients in any and all things in order that they may become. Eliminate any one of the major ingredients and no becoming is possible.

The ability to think of motion as a separate and distinct major ingredient will be difficult for a number of people because of the writings of Aristotle. Aristotle explained motion as the process of potency into act. Which means that in the process of form impressing itself upon common indeterminate matter, there is a by-product called motion which results from this process. Aristotle could not deny or get around the fact of motion, but since he did not consider it as a major necessary ingredient he had to have it as a by-product of, or an accident to, the process of becoming. The result was that he was not able to explain the individuality of becoming. Without an ingredient which allows for an individual becoming, he was forced to place in the form the principle of individuality, and there has been confusion ever since. Form only specifies; it is motion which individualizes a thing. Aristotle used form to explain too many things which form was not capable of explaining,

20

and that is why there is still so much confusion in understanding Aristotle.

Motion determines the personality that each man is given in the state of becoming. Everyone knows that there is a variety of personalities in human nature. Nobody can give an explanation of what brought this variety about if motion is not understood to be a third major ingredient which completes the process of becoming.

The motion that individuates becoming contains the qualities which account for the variety of personalities. Motion contains a given amount of energy and a given quality of energy, and it is this amount and kind which allows for the individuation of the becoming. In the building of a house, it is the skill of the craftsmen that allows the specific house to become. The matter allows for a general becoming, the plans or the design allow for a specific becoming, and now the motion allows for an individual becoming to take place. A house is not a living thing and so the three major ingredients will be different in kind from those of a tree or a man, but they are still the same three ingredients of matter, form and motion. The motion that is necessary for the becoming of a house is that motion which is called skill and talent found in the craftsman. The motion which individuates a becoming human being is called the spirit or the soul of the human person.

Almost everyone will agree that it takes a certain talent to design a building or to direct an army, and not everyone in a society is expected to be able to perform these skills because not everyone has the talent or the personality. This is so because each person has a certain amount and a certain quality of motion which allows for a distinct personality to develop, and this is what allows for individuality in human nature.

We shall see that there are four general presentations of reality and that these presentations correspond to the four causes of reality. There are also four major groupings of personality or human motion. Each group supports one particular cause. The first cause is represented by the

21

warrior group; the second cause is represented by the productive group who form all the social, intellectual and religious institutions; the third group is made up of the ingenious and adaptable personalities who are able to bring forth the fruits from the society; and the last group is made up of the intense and poised persons who bring the society to a finalization and a realization. Each group, as we shall see, has its alloted time and place in the development of mankind and the development of any given civilization or society. In other words, the motion for the entire genius called man is divided in four parts, each part representing the type of motion needed to present that particular cause in reality. This shall be explained and demonstrated more fully as we progress in this work; for the present it is sufficient to say that the total motion of mankind is divided into four groupings in order to present the four causes of reality.

BASIC DIFFERENCE BETWEEN THIS DEMONSTRATION AND ARISTOTLE

It was shown in the beginning of this work that Aristotle reduced Entity to the one ultimate ingredient of form. He admitted that Matter was included in Entity but only in a secondary way, and that the primary and ultimate reduction of the first cause rests upon Form. Aristotle's argument does not explain some basic questions which arise when becoming is considered by itself. Aristotle cannot explain *general becoming*. He cannot say what accounts for the general difference between the animal and the plant or the man and the angel. Unless Aristotle admitted that it is matter which allows for the general or the generic difference of things in becoming, he would never be able to demonstrate and explain what determines becoming in a general manner. Sometimes Aristotle says that it is the form which accounts for the general difference in things, while sometimes he states that it is the combination of matter and form which accounts for the general difference in the becoming of anything. Whichever way he turns he will not be able to explain the general difference of things if form is considered the ultimate ingredient necessary for becoming. The form of Aristotle is considered to be the only active ingredient in the Entity of anything; he considers matter as a passive principle. He has active form acting upon passive matter, and this is supposed to account for becoming. He does not consider the likelihood that both matter and form can be active ingredients, each in its own way.

This idea of the active and the passive really has no bearing upon the problem in the first place. There is nothing active or passive in becoming, for each ingredient plays an active part in the becoming of the thing and each is receptive towards the other ingredients.

Another thing: Aristotle did not make a major distinction between matter, form and motion. He did not consider motion as being a major ingredient and one which is separate and distinct from either matter or form. He perceived motion as being the process of potency to act by the form working upon the matter; when this process took place, motion resulted. In this explanation he can not account for or explain the individuality of things and how individuality takes place in the becoming of anything. In our everyday world of experience we take into account the general as well as the specific and the individual; therefore, something must be held accountable for the general, the specific and the individual in any explanation of reality. What accounts for the general is matter; what accounts for the specific nature of becoming is form. Accordingly, what accounts for the individuality of a thing is motion. In this explanation we have all the major ingredients which our very experience distinguishes unconsciously for us in our daily concern with this reality.

When the explanation of the general, the specific and the individual is put forward, there is no need for confusion and the twisting of theories to account for experienced fact. The rational explanation and the experienced fact become united when each favor the other. In Aristotle, there is no real accounting for the individual in things; the result is the placing upon form the necessity of explaining the species, as well as the individual and the general, through one major ingredient. One ingredient can not handle the whole program, and the result is mental twisting to explain what common sense experience tells us is something other than the explanation given by Aristotle.

PRIORITY OF MATTER . . . THEN FORM . . . THEN MOTION

We have shown that matter determines the general features of becoming. Matter, besides distinguishing as to whether a becoming will be a living or a non-living thing, also determines whether the thing will be in the reality of the angels, the supreme being or man. That is why matter is said to be the first presentation of reality. It is matter which first comes upon the scene and presents some possibility of becoming. The contrary of the first cause is non-reality, and that which is directly opposite non-reality is matter. Matter is the first major ingredient which offers the general possibility of a becoming. That which follows the first major ingredient is the second, form, which specifies what kind of thing the becoming will be. The form specifies whether the becoming will be "this" or "that" kind of plant or animal or man or angel or supreme creator.

It should be remembered that matter represents the general ingredient, and "general" is the broader term and ingredient; thus the broader term will be found in the concepts and ingredients of the specific and the individual, and that is why matter will always be in the specific and in the individual. Nothing can be without matter and nothing can be without form and nothing can be without motion, all three major ingredients being needed at all times. But there is a priority of things or ingredients and it is matter which is needed first, offering the general possibility of becoming. Matter generalizes the becoming thing; form identifies the

24

becoming thing; and motion personalizes the becoming thing, making it an individual and distinct thing.

THE ETERNAL TRINITY FOR ANYTHING

The conclusion from all this is that matter, form and motion must be present at all times in order to have any reality. These three major ingredients have to be present if there is to be a supreme creator; if there are to be angels; if there are to be any men or ducks. These are the three major ingredients in all things, and that is why they can be called the eternal trinity of Matter, Form and Motion. Unless these three major ingredients are eternal, there can be no reality at all. Unless these three be present for all time, it would have to be said that reality comes from nothing; since most sound people will say that reality can't come from non-reality, these three major ingredients have to be present eternally.

Those who hold to the religious doctrine that the supreme creator is composed of three major ingredients often called the Father, the Son and the Holy Spirit are quite correct in their belief, but they should also extend this doctrine to all things in total reality and not confine their belief only to a realm of reality that we are incapable of experiencing. When total reality is understood as being composed of three major ingredients, people will then begin to think in terms of the total oneness, unity and wholeness of the complete reality seen and not seen, experienced and not experienced.

FIRST CAUSE ONLY CONCERNED WITH THE NECESSARY POTENTIAL

The major ingredients of the first cause are only concerned with that which will produce a becoming. They deal with the potential and that is why they can be called the potentials of the first cause. Potential is a very deceptive word, and it can be considered as something that is only possible but not connected with reality. Our concept of the potential includes this idea but it also includes much more; it includes something that is in reality undergoing a process of becoming. This can be illustrated by the example of a house being constructed or a child being formed in the mother. The potential can be the actual becoming or only a possible becoming, but above all it has to do with the "process of becoming" in all its aspects. The potential is only concerned with the first cause and not with any other cause in a precise sense. When we speak of something actual we leave the first cause and enter the second cause, which is concerned with the being of reality. The first cause is only concerned with producing a becoming which, when completed, results in the second cause—the actual being. The end result or the final effect of the becoming is the actual thing.

Any potentiality that is meaningful must offer the possibility of something becoming *general;* of something becoming *specific;* and of something becoming *individual.* The three major ingredients of Entity offer this possibility and this is why Entity is so important in the beginning of this study. Without an understanding of Entity there can be no full understanding of all that is to follow. Once Entity is understood for what it is, the first cause of reality, then the second, third and final causes make more sense.

FOUR WAYS IN WHICH ENTITY IS CONSIDERED

We have said that Entity can be considered in a universal sense when it applies to any possible becoming— past, present or future, or just in the realm of possibility. The universal applies to any becoming and in any tense, and its main concern are the universal requirements of any and all things. We have seen that the universal requirements for any becoming are the major ingredients of matter, form and motion.

When Entity pertains to something actually in the process of becoming, then it is no longer in the region of the universal but in the realm of a general definite reality. When we refer to an actual becoming, we are referring to

26

a becoming taking place in a given realm of reality. Generic matter has decided and determined where a becoming should take place. In other words, some actual matter has provided the material which has determined an actual reality, where a becoming will take place.

Entity can apply to a definite becoming such as Man, or Dog, or Cat; this is the specific becoming of Entity. This is Entity specifying the various kinds of becoming as well as the various kinds of becoming in the species. This specific becoming is concerned with identifying the becoming and distinguishing it from all the other becomings.

When Entity refers to the individual becoming, then it is concerned with the actual "this" common matter; the actual "this" identifying form; and the actual "this" motion. The matter is individual, the form is individual and the motion is individual.

In the universal concept of Entity we are only concerned with that which can be applied to any and all things in any and all reality. In the general concept of Entity we distinguish this realm of reality from any other realm of reality and we distinguish the living from the non-living becoming and we can also distinguish the general types of becoming such as Man, Dog, Sheep or Goat. In the specific realm of Entity we can distinguish the various identifiable becomings besides Man, Dog, etc., but also types within the species, and this is a finer determination of the becoming. Finally, when we get to the individual becoming we are only concerned with some "one" definite becoming. Some "one" definite kind of matter, some "one" definite kind of form and some "one" definite kind of motion. This individual becoming will eventually produce one actual being, and when this happens we enter the second cause of reality —Being.

CHAIN REACTION OF THE THREE MAJOR INGREDIENTS

It was shown that there is a priority of major ingredients with matter the first necessary ingredient, then followed by form and then motion. It should also be pointed out that there is a inter, or intrinsic, and necessary relationship between the three ingredients in which any given one makes no sense without the other two major ingredients always being present. Matter by itself presents a general possibility for a becoming; if there were no form, then nothing could be specified, so what would be the sense of a general becoming? The same holds true if there were only the general possibility and the specific possibility and there was no possibility for an individual becoming; again, what would be the sense of the first two ingredients? All three are necessary to bring forth a becoming into reality and each is necessary to the other two ingredients.

We can see and experience this in our daily lives. Take, for example, the making of bread. It is necessary to have water as the first common ingredient, then flour is needed next and finally motion is needed to stir the flour with the water so that there be some dough to bake the bread. If no motion is applied to the water and the flour there certainly will not be any dough resulting and there will be no bread to bake. Water is necessary, flour is necessary and so is the motion, and each contributes to the becoming of the dough.

All this may sound pretty basic, and so it is, for the beginning of anything should be basic and simple but it should never be taken lightly or for granted for upon the basic and the simple all else rests.

ENTITY THE MATERIAL CAUSE

That which anything rests upon is the material or the foundation supporting the rest of the structure, and this is the context in which the material cause should be considered. Though this cause is composed of three separate and distinct ingredients, these ingredients are of equal necessity and all are considered to be the material foundation which supports the whole structure that is to follow. Once the structure starts to rise, the foundation is covered up and forgotten, and if one has not grasped the basic foundation it is very difficult to support the rest of the structure. It is for this reason that all aspects of the material cause elaborated in this work may seem at times to be repetitious and elementary. It is simple and it is elementary but that is just the point, because it is so simple and elementary that it is often glossed over and not understood; thus when the rest of the structure is built, often there is no foundation to support it.

Entity gives no consideration to the actual, categorical or specified *being*. Being is not in the same cause as Entity. As we shall see, being is concerned with a whole new set of problems which have nothing to do with the material ingredients of the first cause. When Entity has supplied all the major ingredients and these ingredients have produced a becoming of something, and when this becoming is complete, then and only then is the second cause introduced, which is concerned with the development of the reality which presents itself as one being. The final goal of the first cause is to present a one being. When the one being is presented, the second cause begins, which is the formation or development of the being. Nothing in the first cause has anything to do with the formation and the development of a one being. The first cause has all it can do just to present the possibility of the becoming of a "one" being. It's a job in itself to produce a becoming in which the three material ingredients develop to the point that there is presented a complete one being.

MATTER, FORM AND MOTION ALL CONSIDERED MATERIAL IN ENTITY

The three major ingredients of matter, form and motion are all material ingredients of the first cause. Since only the potential or the becoming is considered in the first cause, anything that is in this cause falls under the general classification of material. There is no definition of actual, categorical being which is able to be identified in the first cause since only the becoming is presented. No one thing has been

29

established and no identity or organization of anything has been presented, for no stable definition can be achieved in the state of becoming. In becoming there is only a process leading to the state of being, and in this process all is in a state or flux and no full definition can be given of the reality at this phase of its development. We may know that the becoming thing may eventually be a man, or a woman, or a sheep, or a tree, but while in the state of becoming there is not presented the "actual" one being, and for this reason no definite form can be given to the thing. The form means not only the outside form of the thing but the complete formation of the thing as a one identifiable thing which has a definite identity and which has established a definite operation. This will be explained fully in the second cause; for the present it is necessary to establish the fact that only the material consideration is considered in the first cause and for this reason the first cause takes on a colorless tone with no definite shape or size. We can observe this when a building is in a stage of construction—all is in a stage of confusion and flux. We see material arriving at the job site and people with plans in their hands and we see the skilled men erecting the material into some vague shape—but nothing is definite. The designer may know what the building will eventually look like but there is still no actual building which has a definite shape and operation. This is what Entity is all about: the first presentation of something real, and all that is concerned with, is the major basic material so that there can be this presentation of the first stage of reality.

ALL THINGS ARE CONSIDERED AS FORM IN THE SECOND CAUSE

The first cause was interested in establishing a becoming and that is why all the ingredients are called and placed under the material classification. The fact that they are called ingredients indicates this. Anything that appears in the second cause will fall under the classification of formation. This formation will not be concerned with ingredients but with principles of development. These principles are not concerned with the becoming of the thing but with the development or the formation of the "one" presented being. This is what the second cause is all about, then, the formation and the development of the effect of the first cause.

What was the ultimate effect of the first cause? It was the presentation of a "one" thing and that is all that it was required to do—present to reality a "one" thing. When we study the second cause, what we will be considering are the formation and development of this "one" thing which the Entity has presented to the reality. Then we will be considering the "one" thing. Then we will be considering the identity of this one being and then the operation of this identified being. But all this is in the second cause which is concerned with the development and the formulation of the presented thing.

ALL THINGS ARE CONSIDERED IN TERMS OF FRUITION IN THE THIRD CAUSE

When we have considered the formation and the development of the being, we then leave the second cause and enter the third cause, in which all things will be considered in terms of efficiency and fruition. Everything in the third cause will fall under the classification of motion fruition. In the third cause we will not be interested in the possible or the potential of the reality, so we will not be interested in the material aspects of the thing. What we will be interested in are the fruits that the thing produces, and so our concern will be with the efficiency of the thing as to the amount and the quality of the fruits which the thing produces. Any and all things that fall within the classification of the third cause will come under the general heading of Motion or production.

THE FOURTH CAUSE IS ONLY CONCERNED WITH THE FINAL PURPOSE

After something becomes, after it has developed itself and after it has produced some fruits, the next and the last question that is asked is what is the purpose of the thing in the first place? The purpose means the finalization and the realization of the thing. We are now concerned with the ultimate completed thing as it can be achieved in the reality in which it finds itself. We won't be talking about the potential or about the actual or about the idealized; what we will be talking about is the realized and completed thing as it can be presented in the reality in which it finds itself. This final cause is not concerned with the termination of the thing but with the ultimate accomplishment of the thing, than which nothing more can be achieved.

Anything falling within this classification can be considered only in the light of the finalized reality. The thing has realized its fullest capabilities and nothing more follows after the fourth cause. This realization takes the same length of time to accomplish as the other three causes. It is concerned with its own set of problems and solutions just as the other three causes are, and although the reality enter the fourth cause, this has nothing to do with the termination of reality. It simply means the completion of the thing. When something is complete it does not mean that something must end or terminate. Just the opposite is implied, for a completed reality means that all things should be in a harmony, working together and not in a state of chaos and confusion.

SUMMATION OF THE CAUSES

In each cause we will have considered four different sets of problems and also four different sets of questions. Each cause will have emphasized a separate and distinct set of terms, with four different languages being involved to express their full reality. Materiality will be the language of the first cause, and the viewpoint will be through the potential. Formality will be the language of the second cause, for we will be interested in the development and the formation of the actual being and concerned with the determination of the reality. In the third cause the language will be in terms of efficiency and the production of fruits from the developed reality. We will be talking in terms of efficiency and production and will use the language of the distribution of the fruits of the production, and we will be looking out upon reality in an ideal way so that we can best find more suitable ways and means of increasing the fruits and the production of the reality. In the last cause our language will be in terms of the realized thing. We will be looking at reality from the view that the reality has achieved its practical realization, and our language will be concerned with the oneness and the harmony of the completed reality. The first language is paternalistic. The second language is classical and intellectual. The third language is idealistic and romantic. The fourth language is practical and realistic.

MATERIALITY STRESSED BY THE EARLY GREEK THINKERS

The earliest Greek thinkers stressed the material viewpoint of reality. As Greek culture grew, the first phase was passed and a new phase of the second cause replaced the emphasis upon the material. Thus the formal viewpoint was expressed by such thinkers as Aristotle and his followers. This was followed by thinkers who stressed the view of what the life of a man should produce and who concerned themselves with the virtues and the values of the productive life. This was the view of Plato and his followers. In the last period of Greek culture the summation and the realization of the whole thinking process was the main goal society concentrated upon.

To understand reality in all its manifestations, all the causes must be considered and each cause must be given its due consideration. It must be remembered that it is natural for a thinker who is emphasizing a new cause over the one that has been in development in the society for generations to deride and to make light of the former cause. The former cause has played itself out and is given lip service by the leading thinkers of the new age.

The early period of Greek culture stressed the material ingredients of water, air, fire and earth as the important factors of reality. Aristotle stressed the second cause, and naturally he emphasized the formal consideration of the reality and de-emphasized the material ingredients. Plato stressed the productivity or the fruitfulness of the individual person. Thus there had to be a necessary disagreement between Aristotle and Plato.

Motion had been introduced for the first time as a separate and distinct major ingredient, along with matter and form, and it was quite natural to stress motion over matter and the form. As this was done, the emphasis turned upon the third cause, with a corresponding de-emphasis of the other two causes. This should not be done if a true understanding of all the causes are to be achieved. Each cause is important for the full presentation of reality. However, each cause is given more emphasis at one period then the other three, for there is a time and place for each cause to fully develop and present its facet of reality.

The materiality of the first cause provides the opportunity for something to become generally possible. This in turn provides the need to have something specifically determined and thus the need for the form to specify the being. The motion of the third cause is needed to provide the energy to allow the fruition of the individual thing. This in turn leads to the finalization of the reality, which is the fourth cause. This is a good example of why the various thinkers should be judged not upon their overall viewpoint of reality but upon which cause they emphasized. It is almost impossible for one person to completely emphasize all four causes to their fullest degree. We shall see that in the history of thought, in the history of governments and in the history of religions, there are four separate and distinct periods, each representing one definite cause; it would be natural that there would be one outstanding personality in each of the periods who best sums up the period and the cause. There is the courageous chieftain of the first period who battles to bring all the major ingredients together. The scholar and thinker of the second period formulates and gives identity to the society. The inventor and the scientist and the producer of goods of the third period brings forth the fruits of the society. The leader brings about the realization and the finalization of the society in the fourth period. Each period calls for a distinct personality to bring about its completion.

In the historical setting, it takes a courageous personality to bring about a becoming, for the three major ingredients must be brought together so that there can be one becoming society. The becoming of any given society takes about 500 years, almost exactly, as the historical record will show.

ENTITY IS POTENTIAL, NOT ACTUAL

Nothing is completely determined in the becoming of Entity. Entity concerns itself with the becoming, the potential, the possible, the probable. A becoming is something real, it is happening and it is the first presentation of reality, but it is not something that is actually presented. When we use the term "actually," we mean something that is fully developed and fully presented. The providing of the becoming is the purpose of entity. Without the possibility of a becoming, there can be no possibility of an actual determined thing. The first presentation is the most important of the causes in order of priority, for without it the rest of the causes could not come forth. It can be seen that the first cause is the father of the other three, for it allows reality to come forth. To offer the first chance to reality is something of no mean importance. Without a chance of becoming there is no need for the rest of the causes. The first cause offers the beginning to reality, but receives little or no recognition in the field of philosophy.

The rational faculties are concerned with the categorial interpretations of reality and with the actual understanding of the determined thing. The rational faculties are not concerned with the undetermined and becoming reality. Entity is the forgotten child of the intellectual, for entity

35

occurs in the historical setting of the pioneer days of the society. Entity is concerned with the days when epic poems were being composed. Entity concerns the days of the founding fathers of a civilization during the dark ages of its becoming. In the world historical setting, entity occurs during the pre-historic ages. This was the period in which the human race was in the state of becoming. Once this period was completed, mankind entered the period of being, which is concerned with the second cause of reality.

Contemporary psychologists have shown that there is a thing called the "id" in the psychic nature of man. This "id" is something that is cloudy and lies at the bottom of the consciousness of any man. It is related to the becoming part of man and to man's Entity. It lies below the rational or the conscious understanding of reality. It supports the conscious area of the human psyche. Because it is the becoming phase of the human psyche it is cloudy, murky, undetermined, and has the potential for anything. Deep-seated desires and drives originate there, for this is the becoming of all things. This "id" represents the dark ages of human development, and when the society places too much emphasis upon the second and the third cause, the "id" manifests itself in the oddest and the most uncomfortable way to let us know that we came from a becoming that was cloudy, dark and murky.

The "ego" is the formal realm or the classificational area in a person's psyche. The "ego" is based upon the second cause of reality and thus the "ego" is the determining factor in the psyche of a person. The "ego" is concerned with reason and the intellectual categorization of reality. It is the area of being. The ego is concerned with the consciousness of the person and the determined reality that is presented to the person.

The third area in the psyche life of the person is that of the "superego." This is the realm based upon the third cause of reality. It is concerned with the motivation and the energy required to produce something from the being. It strives to accomplish the fruition of the being. This is the area in which the person dreams and strives towards some ideal which he wishes to produce from his own being. It is the area in which a person wishes to produce in himself a similar model of some ideal person or achievement. It is the area of the psyche which produces the fruits of the personality.

A fourth area of the human psyche is that which is based upon the fourth cause, and this area may be called the "perfected psyche." Its purpose is to allow the person to become one with the reality in which he finds himself, to achieve a harmony with the reality and to become a part of the whole. This is the mature psyche. Its purpose is to consider the individual with the whole of the reality and to allow the individual to participate as an integral part of the whole and in a way that is favorable to the person and to the whole of reality.

The four causes are represented in any facet of reality to which one may wish to refer. We may inter-relate the facets and the causes if we wish. For example, the Substrate, the "id" and the dark ages are all in the area of the first cause. All these terms refer to an area in which becoming takes place. In the second cause we refer to the Substance, the "ego," the Middle Ages, in which the development of the being and the development of the identity of the thing takes place. In the third cause we refer to the Illuminated Ideal, the super-picture of the super-ideal man of the Renaissance. The super-ego and the super-productive person is now the rage of the day, and so has begun the emphasis upon the fruitional facet of reality and the productive side of man's nature. After this period has passed we will enter the area of the fourth cause, in which the emphasis will be upon the Substantial, the perfected psyche, the realized reality and the practical realization of reality.

ENTITY THE START

It was expressed by Aristotle that the highest type of knowledge is the knowledge acquired through the understanding of the concept of entity. This statement is as true today as the day it was first uttered. The understanding of entity is one of the most difficult, and yet it is one of the most rewarding. Entity is the start of the understanding of reality. To know what is necessary for a becoming is to understand the basic requirements for any and all reality. If entity is thought to include only one major ingredient, such as form, then the whole outlook upon the rest of reality will also be colored and slanted toward form. If entity is thought to consist only of matter, then all that follows will be biased towards the material side of reality. If entity is understood as having only one or two major ingredients, there will arise the conception of nature revolving around the one major ingredient or revolving around the dualistic conception of nature. When entity is understood correctly as having three major ingredients, then one's view of reality assumes a different perspective.

ETERNITY OF THE TRINITY

In order to have any reality at all it is necessary to have the three major ingredients. Since nothing can come from nothing and since we are faced with something called reality, there must be the three major ingredients present beyond the realm of any particular time. The realm that is not concerned with the particular is called eternity. If matter were missing there would be no need for form and, if form and matter were missing there would be no need for motion. In other words, all three things must be present in order to have reality. This is what is meant by the eternity of the three major ingredients or the eternity of the primary trinity. Regardless of when this reality that we experience came about, there had to be something prior to this particular reality because it had a becoming and the three major ingredients had to support this becoming. That is why matter, form and motion per se had to be present before this particular becoming or it would not be possible to have this reality, or any reality.

REALITY FOR ARISTOTLE

Aristotle's reality was one in which the highest perfection consisted of a perfect order, with no becoming, no production, no fruitification and no complete realization. Ultimately it was a reality of pure order and pure categorical immobility. The concept of the unmoved mover as the highest achievement and ultimate accomplishment of this conception is well known. Aristotle's emphasis was solely upon the second cause of reality. Plato, on the other hand, concentrated upon the third cause and emphasized the ultimate achievement as coming as close as possible to producing the perfect ideal in this reality. The perfect ideal was the ultimate perfection of the singular human being patterned after the eternal illuminated ideal. The highest achievement for Plato was the person who was motivated towards perfecting himself after the illuminated ideal which was eternal and presented itself to those men who prepared themselves to receive the illuminated ideal.

No one can say that Aristotle was wrong and no one can say that Plato was wrong. Each ultimately was emphasizing one definite cause to the exclusion of others. The causes that each emphasized have never been excelled by any other thinker and that is why these two thinkers continue on through the ages. These thinkers built their systems upon the solid bedrock of a definite cause, producing a definite effect. That is why they continue to interest mankind. The purpose of this work is not to place emphasis upon one or two causes but to show the interrelationship of all four causes; we wish to show the whole forest and not just a patch of it.

The problem of matter has led many towards wrong conclusions in the field of philosophy. The Greeks concentrated so heavily upon the form of things that the idea persists to this very day with many thinkers that anything not connected with matter is something of a spiritual nature and therefore of greater value than that which is composed of matter of some kind.

The ideal tree or the ideal man or the ideal angel or the ideal God can have a form or design independent of any reality through the energy of the mind making an illuminated ideal and concentrating upon the third cause. The illuminated ideal can thus be easily disconnected from becoming, from being and from realization, which are all products or effects of the first, second and fourth causes. The minute reality enters the picture some kind of matter becomes unionized with the ideal form. The tree can have a reality, other than the reality that we experience, by changing the "matter" which offers the potential for the tree. A man can live in a reality other than the one that he is now in by only changing the "kind of" matter which is associated with this reality. The difference between the ideal and the real is matter, and this literally makes all the difference in the world.

A universal ideal of an animal and the fact of a real animal is the difference between having matter and not having matter. The real animal has matter (as well as form and motion), while the illuminated ideal animal is one composed from the ingenuity of the mind based upon fragments found in reality. Nothing is wrong with this, but to say that something is more real if it does not have matter or motion is a fault which persists down to our times because of the emphasis given the third cause to the exclusion of the other three causes.

Angels, demons and all other kindred spirits, along with the supreme creator, must have some kind of matter or they can not be real. What places them in different realms of reality is the matter that first offers them the possibility of becoming. A supreme being may never go through the process of becoming, but he must have the three major material ingredients. This is the first cause, and the first cause is dealing with becoming. Everything must have a becoming, but everything need not go through the process of becoming.

Matter is not something that is purely passive, as Aristotle claimed. Matter determines the reality that a certain

40

potentiality is to take place in. It may be considered passive when it is receptive to a form, but in the fullest sense it offers just as much determination as the other two major material ingredients. Matter provides the general determination, while form provides the specific determination and motion the individual determination. Each has a specific area of determination, and one can not do without the other.

BARE BONES OF THE FIRST CAUSE

We have shown that the first cause is concerned with bringing about a becoming of one definite thing. After this one definite thing has become, then there is no longer a need for the first cause because its effect has already been accomplished. There is a definite effect to each cause. Once this has been accomplished the need for the cause is over. But the effect brings about the need for the next cause. So the second cause will be concerned with the formation or the development of the effect that was produced by the first cause. This formation or development is concerned with the being of a thing. Entity is what the first cause is all about; being is what the second case is all about. The first cause is concerned with producing one determined entity. The second cause is concerned with producing one developed being.

II. THE SECOND PRESENTATION
OF REALITY

The second cause of reality has four separate and distinct groupings, as does the first cause. The groupings of the first cause were: 1. Entity; 2. The Potential; 3. The Substrate; 4. Matter, Form, and Motion. These four groupings correspond to the four causes inherent in each presentation of reality. These four causes permeate all phases of reality. Anything that one may be talking about will contain the four causes. One is not able to avoid these concepts, for they are that which makes up the very nature of things. Each cause by itself has something different and special to say about reality. That is why, in the first cause, the four causes present themselves, as we have shown, through the entity, potential, substrate, and matter-form-motion. So, in the second cause, the four causes will present themselves through: 1. Being; 2. Actual; 3. Substance; 4. Essence, and Operation. Notice that we have a similar arrangement of parts as in the first presentation. There is one great difference, though. In the first presentation we were concerned with the material ingredients necessary for the becoming of one definite thing. In the second presentation we will be concerned with the *principles* necessary for the development of the being.

In the first presentation of reality only the potential was considered, and this dealt with a becoming which was trying to effect a one determined thing. Now, in the second cause, this one determined thing has been effected and we are going to be concerned with the development and the formation of the being so that it will be fully actual and developed. As potency was concerned with the becoming of the entity so that there would be effected a one determined thing, so actuality is going to be concerned with the development of the being so that there is effected a one whole and complete being.

What is actually developed in our realm of experience is the form of being called substances. Beings which we are not able to experience are something other than substances. An angel or a demon or some other thing that is not composed of the matter of reality is not a being presented to our experience and thus is not a substance. Those things which are actually presented and developed in our realm of reality are called substances.

THREE PARTS TO THE DEVELOPMENT OF BEINGS WHICH WE EXPERIENCE

The individual beings which we experience are developed through three parts. These three parts of the being are the three major principles: 1. Essence; 2. Existence; 3. Operation. Essence is concerned with the development of the oneness of being. Existence is concerned with the development of the unity and identity of being. Operation is concerned with the development of the completeness of being.

THE FOUR CAUSES PRESENTED IN THE SECOND CAUSE

The second presentation of reality is divided into four groups corresponding to the four causes found in all things. Being is related to the material cause, for being is that which offers the potential for development in the second cause. Actuality is related to the formal cause, because full development occurs only in the actual presented being. Substance is related to the efficient cause, for it is the substance which is specifically to be completed and developed in this cause. Essence, existence and operation are related to the final cause, for these are the three principles which allow the individual thing to be completely developed.

In the second presentation we will be dealing with something that has achieved its one determination and is now trying to effect full development. The effect of the full development of its oneness is what actuality is concerned with. A becoming considers the bringing together of the three major ingredients so that there will be effected a one determined thing. This is all considered in the realm of the potential. After the one determined thing has been effected, the development of this one thing to its fullest extent is what actuality is all about. To bring about the full development of an actual substance, the full development of the essence achieves a one developed thing. The full development of the existence achieves the unity of the thing with the reality which allows for the full identity of the thing. Finally, the full development of the operation of the thing allows for the completeness of the thing. These terms will be covered fully later on in this chapter.

ACTUALITY IS THE OPPOSITE OF POTENTIAL

The second cause of reality is one step removed from non-reality. Entity is opposite non-reality, and potential is opposite nothing or non-becoming; so, in the second presentation, what is opposite actuality is becoming. We know that becoming is the process in which major ingredients are bringing about a oneness of something. When this oneness is achieved, the necessity then is to develop this oneness to the fullest extent possible. Thus, actuality starts from a one determined thing and develops that determined thing to the fullest extent possible.

ACTUAL BEING

A being cannot be potential—either it is a determined one thing or it is not a being. The potential or the possible is in the realm of the first cause. The determined one thing, the thing presented via the first cause, is the object which

44

will be developed in the second cause. The full development will try to take place in the second cause. In the second cause, the being is not asked to become a determined thing, nor is it asked to produce something from its being. What is asked of the reality in the second cause is to develop the actual reality presented through the first cause. Actuality refers to the general state in which the development of the being is taking place. The oneness is developing, the unity and the identity are developing, and the being completes his development through the operation of his being.

Actuality, then, is not a static state in which development and determination have been achieved; rather, it is the state in which the development is being achieved. It is the period of the growth of the being developing itself to the fullest extent possible. What has been achieved by the becoming of the first cause is developed by the second cause.

SPECIFIC BEING

Actual being specifies the kind of being that is to develop. What is specified in our realm of reality are beings that are called substances. These are the beings which are specifically to be developed in the second cause of reality. Substances are those beings which have developed from the becoming of the first cause. One major ingredient by itself can not be considered as a substance. Water, which is one of the major ingredients for all living things, cannot by itself produce a substance. A living substance must have, besides water, a determining design which is found in the blood or the seed of the living thing, and there must be some quality of motion which makes the living thing a singular living thing. Three major ingredients contribute to the substance. This is the specified being which is to be developed in the second cause. Water, earth, or the other ingredients making up this world, are not substances because they do not go through a process of development. Water is water; it does not develop nor does it produce something from itself. Only in substances is the oneness produced from the becoming developed, and this is the specific thing that is to be developed in the second cause.

THE INDIVIDUAL BEING

The individual being that is to be developed in the second cause is known through its essence, existence and operation. These are the three principles through which the individual development takes place. Notice that we have said principles and not ingredients. Ingredients are found in the first cause, principles are found in the second cause, values will be found in the third cause and goals will be found in the fourth cause.

The individual is developed through the principles of essence, existence and operation, and these are the areas through which development will take place in the second cause. Many people have heard it said that essence is that which makes a thing what it is. Most have accepted this definition and proceeded along their way. But the definition does not really tell us anything, and in a certain sense it is definitely not correct. Substance is what it is not through the essence but through the becoming of the three major ingredients of the first cause. When it reaches the second cause, the essence is concerned with the development of the whatness. Essence means the development of the one thing to its fullest extent. What the thing is has been achieved in the becoming, for this has produced a one being. The oneness of this being is what the principle of essence is all about. In an individual living substance, this means the development of the matter, the form and the motion to its fullest possible extent. This achievement is through the principle of essence. Essence is the principle of oneness in the substance. This principle is developed in the second cause of reality.

In man, the principle of oneness is concerned with three areas; the material or physical; the formal or intellectual; and the religious or spiritual. These are the three major areas in which oneness is achieved in the individual man.

46

Essence is something dynamic and moving. It is not something that has simply determined a being and nothing more. Each thing in each of the causes is in a state of development and nothing remains fixed and completely immovable. Because many people have confused essence with the state of becoming it was often thought that essence had to do with the major ingredients. This cannot be the case. First of all, by the very definition of essence—that which makes a thing what it is—this definition refers to a one thing. The one thing is not found in the first cause, for the first cause is in the process of producing the one thing. Only at the very end of the first cause, in the ultimate effect of the first cause, is the one thing found. When it is found, one immediately goes into the second cause, the development of the one thing. What makes a thing to be one are the three major ingredients of matter, form and motion. What develops this one thing is the principle of essence. This principle develops the one thing to its fullest extent, and this is what essence is all about.

EXISTENCE

Besides developing the one being to its fullest possible extent, it is necessary to develop the identity of the being. This is accomplished through the principle of existence. Many people have heard the word existence mentioned. Naturally there have been very few definitions given as to what is meant by existence. We wish to state here that it is the second principle in the development of the individual being and is concerned with establishing an identity or unity with the being and with the reality in which the being finds itself.

We have a very good example of what existence is all about in our day and age. There is much discussion and aggravation over the lack of communication between peoples and generations. Because of the lack of communication between the youth and the older people, there is a search for identity on the part of the young and a grieving on the part of the older generation for its inability to communicate with the younger generation. All this has to do with the principle of existence. This is what existence is all about. It is the development of being so that the being is able to unite itself with the reality in which it finds itself. This union enables an identity to be formed and developed in the being. When there is a lack of communication or a breakdown of communication there is an inability for the younger developing being to become identified and unified with the reality in which he finds himself. The result is the search for identity and unity among the youth of this and other lands.

Another example of existence is the problem that the U.S. is having with the race issue. The Negro race has not really been in communication with the white majority and consequently has not formed an identity with the white community. Because its leading members wish to become identified with the reality in which they find themselves, they are seeking ways in which to communicate with the reality, some by peaceful means and others by violent means. The objective is the same, though, the desire and the need to communicate with and to be united with the reality in which they find themselves. This is what the principle of existence tries to accomplish.

Another reason why there is a lack of communication between youth and the older generation has to do with the viewpoint of the two groups. The youth is in a period of development and its views are those of the second cause, which is concerned with the development of the oneness of the being, the establishment of the identity of the being and the achievement of the complete operation of the being. The views of the older generation are concentrated upon the third and the fourth cause, and this is why there is a general lack of communication, along with the fact that the world is in a period of transition from the third cause to the fourth cause. But all this is taking us too far away from our main subject—the development of the individual through the principle of existence. All we should say now

48

about world affairs and the principle of existence is that every time a civilization goes through a period of transition, there is a breakdown in communication between the youth, who represent the new cause entering the society, and the older generation, which still supports the old cause. This has happened in ancient times. It has happened in the period between the Dark Ages and the Middle Ages, between the Middle Ages and our present age which began with the Renaissance and is now coming to an end. So we are having the same breakdown in communication between those who still follow the old viewpoint and the youth who are trying to find the words to express the views of the coming age. There are a great number of writers and thinkers who have commented upon the existential plight of the modern man, so we need not say more than was and is better said by the writers and thinkers of our present age. All this because the principle of existence is somewhat frustrated in those beings who are developing in the second cause of reality.

There has been a whole history of books concerning the so-called problem of essence and existence, and it seems to me that more cloudy information has been given than clear. All this has been the result of a lack of understanding of what is meant by cause and what each cause is trying to accomplish. Now, besides our two principles of essence and existence in the second cause there is also a third principle called operation. None of these principles are in conflict with each other. Each has a definite function to perform and each in a way is dependent upon the other.

Besides trying to develop a oneness through the essence, and besides trying to unify and identify the being with itself and with its reality, the third principle of operation tries to complete the being by giving it a place in the reality and having it face a certain set of circumstances. This operation allows the being to have a completeness with itself and with the reality in which it finds itself. That is why those beings that do not have a place in the system in which they find themselves and who are not faced with a definite set of circumstances feel somehow that they are not complete. And it is true, they are not complete beings because their principle of operation has been frustrated.

In the second cause we have covered the universal term, being. We have also covered the general term, which is the actual presented thing. We have covered the specific thing presented for development, which is substance. We have now introduced the three principles which will be concerned with the development of the individual being.

These three principles each contain three parts. The total of these parts result in the nine categories of the individual being.

THE CATEGORIES

It is through the categories that the second cause develops its effect. The first three categories concern themselves with developing the essence of the being. The second three categories bring about the unity and identity of the being. The third three categories allow for the completeness of the being to develop.

The three categories in the essence are quantity, quality and relationship. These categories are based upon the three major ingredients, as are all the other categories. Quantity is based upon matter; quality is based upon the form; and the relationship between the two is based upon motion. It can be seen that there is an interconnection between all the aspects of the four causes. These three categories bring about the full development of the oneness of the being. When this is applied to man, the quantity is the physical development of the man; the the quality is the intellectual development; and the relationship is the spiritual development. The total allows for the full oneness of the man. In a society this is translated into institutions which are concerned with the three categories of oneness. Government is concerned with the physical development of the human person; the schools are concerned with the intellectual development of the being; and the churches are concerned

50

with the spiritual development of the person. All governments are concerned with the distribution of the material goods of the land as well as the physical health of the population. The schools are interested in the intellectual quality of the people and the development of the talents of the people. The churches are concerned with the conduct of relationships among the people and the relationship of the people with the other realms of reality. These are the three categories of the essence as found in the society of man.

SECOND THREE CATEGORIES

The second three categories are concerned with bringing about the unity and identity of the being. They are based also upon the three major ingredients of matter, form and motion. The three categories of existence are: receptivity, activity and time. Receptivity is based on or related to matter; activity is related to form, and time is related to motion.

What is to be accomplished in these three categories is the uniting of the being with the reality in which it finds itself so that some identity can be formed. The material by which the being is surrounded is receptive to the developing being. The material in the being is receptive to the reality surrounding it. Thus, matter is receptive to matter. The activity of the reality surrounding the being acts upon the being. The activity of the being acts upon the surrounding reality. Activity forms the reality. The activity of the reality forms the being and the activity of the being forms the reality.

The last category of existence is that of time. Time is based upon motion. The surrounding reality has a certain degree of motion. The developing being also has a certain degree of motion. The degree of motion in the surrounding reality individuates the being and the degree of motion in the developing being individuates the reality around it. A little confusing? If so, it is because so far no one has given a good definition of what time is all about.

Time, as we said, is based upon motion. There are certain degrees of motion for any given specie. Each being, when it begins to develop, starts with a certain degree of motion. The development of man and of most animals starts when they are born. The first cause takes place inside the mother and the second cause begins when man is born. When a person is born he enters into a certain degree of motion at the instant that he is born. The reality into which the infant is born contains at that instant a definite degree of motion. This degree of motion the infant acquires at birth, and it is the degree in which the infant develops. This degree of motion is called time. The whole energy-making apparatus of mankind contains all the degrees of motion which give variety to human nature. Variety in human nature, or in any living nature, comes about when the being is born into a certain period of time. This time is a period or degree of motion. A being given a certain degree of motion produces a variety; the degree of motion in one being is different from the degree of motion of any other being because of the different times in which each was born.

This degree of motion produces a distinct kind of energy in each being and this is how the identity of the being is developed. Thus, since matter is receptive to matter and the activity is forming the surrounding reality and forming the being, what is needed is a degree of motion which will individuate the general receptivity with the formal or specific activity so that one identity can be formed. This is exactly what is accomplished in the existence of the being. This is also how the personality of the person develops. Each being has a degree of time due to the time in which he was born. This allows the being to exert a certain degree of motion, which produces a definite personality in existence.

The birth day, besides beginning the second cause of the human being, is also the day that the being acquires the degree of motion that is prevailing at the time. Thus, a person born in the winter months or the beginning months of the year will have one kind of personality while those born during the spring, summer and fall will all have different kinds of personality. As there are four major causes, so there are four major personality groupings. Each group stresses one of the major causes. Each cause takes a certain kind and degree of energy in which to complete its effect, and that is why there are four major types of personality in mankind. It all depends on which cause was prevailing in the world at the time that the being was born.

We have alluded to the fact that each cause has its period of time in which it works itself out in reality before the next cause takes its place. A being born into a given cause receives the degree of motion or energy of that cause. All we will say in this respect is that each cause is provided with nine different degrees so that there is a total of nine personalities in each cause, with a total of thirty-six personalities for the whole of mankind. By personalities we mean thirty-six degrees of motion allowing for that many basic personalities. If someone should think that this is not enough for the whole of mankind, they should stop and think a minute. Each person receives something definite from the reality in which he finds himself. No two beings are receptive to the same thing. Nor are any two beings active upon the same thing. So the degree of motion applied at the time allows for a distinct personality to form. The personality and the degrees of motion will be taken up more thoroughly in the third cause; for the present it is only necessary to know that the time is the period which specifies the degree of motion which the person is using to identify himself.

So far we have seen that in the second cause, the principle of essence is concerned with developing the oneness of the being. In the human being this means developing the physical, the intellectual and the spiritual or religious areas of the human being so that they form one being, or better yet, so that they form one human being. In the first cause the becoming was trying to develop a being and in the second cause the development of the being is trying to

53

produce a human being. So, besides the principle of essence, there is the principle of existence, which allows for the identification of the human being. Last but not least is needed a principle of operation which will allow for the completeness of the being.

OPERATION

The principle of operation is concerned with developing the completeness of the being so that the being participates in the activity of the reality in which it finds itself, so that the being has a place in the reality in which it finds itself and, finally, so that the being can face a certain set of circumstances.

Operation allows for the being to become completely involved in the reality in which it finds itself. Operation consists of three parts. These three parts, as we have seen, are related to the three major ingredients of the first cause. The three parts of the operational principle are the regular acts of the being or its habits; the place or the position in which the being finds itself; and the circumstances surrounding the being at the time that he is born and begins his operation.

The surrounding reality performs certain definite actions and acts. These are the habits of the society into which a human is born, or they may be the regular activities of nature for other animals or plants and living things. These regular activities allow the being to become involved in the reality because the being also begins to have regular activities which become interrelated with the activities of the reality. This allows for the being to add some completeness to the reality in which it finds itself and also to complete the being of itself.

Besides engaging in the regular activities of the reality there is a place or position for the being in the reality in which it finds itself. This place or position allows for the efficient operation of the whole reality. Place and position allow for the basic of authority in human and other animal societies. Place or position allows the new being to have a part in the completeness of the reality. A being that has no place in the society is not able to fully complete its being. This is the reason why there is so much disturbance in human society; there simply is no place for a vast number of people, not because of overpopulation but because of poor social structure.

To complete a being it is necessary to have regular activities performed by the being and to have a place for the being to occupy in the reality in which he finds himself. It is also necessary for the being to be faced with a set of circumstances in which he will be able to operate. If a being performs regular acts in the society and if he has a place in the reality in which he finds himself, but if he is not able to act upon the circumstances which are present to him, the being finds that he does not have complete operation. There is nothing more frustrating than performing some activity in the society and having a place in the society but not being able to act upon the circumstances with which one is faced in the reality. It is the regular activities of the being and the place in which the being finds itself and the set of circumstances upon which the being is capable of acting that completes the being and accounts for the full development of the being.

We have now completed the development of the being. The three categories of the essence are concerned with the development of the oneness of the being. The development of the oneness concerns the developing to the fullest possible extent the quantity of the being, the quality of the being and the relationship of the being. In the human being this revolves around the physical, the intellectual and the spiritual. In any given society there are corresponding institutions for this purpose. Governments take care of the physical or material; schools take care of the intellectual and the churches take care of spiritual and the moral relationships of the people.

The next three categories are concerned with the development of the identity of the person. This is achieved through the receptivity of the being to the reality; through the activity of the being and the reality; through the time which contains a definite degree and intensity of motion allowing for an identity to develop which is separate and distinct from all other identities of the same specie. This allows for variety to be achieved in nature or in reality.

The last three categories are concerned with developing the completeness of the being and the reality in which the being finds itself. By performing regular actions with the reality and by having a place in the reality and by acting upon a given set of circumstances, it allows for the complete being to develop in the reality and for the being to complete the reality in which it is participating.

In the second cause we have the three principles of essence, existence and operation through which the being develops, and in these principles are the nine categories. The three categories in each principle enable the being to develop to the fullest extent possible, and this is what the second cause is all about. If one reads much philosophy one might easily assume that this study concerns itself with the static and the completed. We can see, however, when the true presentation of reality is understood, that the whole of philosophy is concerned with the pulsating, living, dynamic development of reality. Nothing is static or completely fixed and finished. Everything is always in a state of development. Each cause has something definite to accomplish, and when in man or in a society or in a civilization the one cause has produced its effect, the reality moves on to the next cause, and this is what we shall do also.

III. THE THIRD PRESENTATION OF
REALITY: THE FRUITION
OF THINGS

We have seen that in the first cause the emphasis was upon the material ingredients which allow a becoming to take place. Thus the first cause is rightly called the material cause. We have seen that the purpose of the second cause is to develop or formalize the being. This is rightly called the formal cause of reality, and that is why the formal development is concerned with the categories in which the formation of the thing is allowed to take place. Now, in the third cause, we are going to be considering the fruits that come forth from the being. Our emphasis, therefore, will be upon the production of the individual thing and upon the efficiency of the thing. We have seen that in all things there is an inter-relationship of parts and attributes, and this can be applied to the understanding of the causes in this manner: We have seen that in the first cause we were concerned with the general becoming of something, and that it what the material stressed. We have seen in the second cause that the development of the being was emphasized, and this emphasis was upon the species of the thing as distinguished from the general becoming of the first cause. This is what the categories are all about, they specify the various ways in which the being is to become formalized. Therefore, the emphasis upon the species is the predominant factor in this cause. No one expects children to produce anything for they are in the state of development. Now, in the third cause, what we are going to be interested in is just this—the production of things from the being.

The emphasis now flows from the general to the specific and then into individual thing.

We have seen that the opposite of non-reality was the possible or potential reality of the first cause. The possible enables a new becoming to take place. Opposite to the becoming in our march to reality is the development of the being. This is the concentration upon the specific thing and the categorization and the stabilization of the being. Now, contrary or opposite to the second cause is the dynamic, energetic and efficient viewpoint of the third cause. This is the cause that looks upon reality not from the viewpoint of the stability of the society but from the viewpoint of producing something from the reality. So the emphasis in reality is now upon the energy to produce something, the movement or motion needed to produce goods and products.

To accomplish the production of something or to bring forth something from being there must be presented some general ideal or idea by which the person strives to release energy or motion so that the production of something will be accomplished. This general ideal or idea is often presented as something in which the being should strive to attain.

This is sometimes given as the better way of life, or the better society or the better world in which the person would be living if he produced some goods or made something of himself. This making something of the self is the ideal after which the being strives and is the general purpose of the third cause—to get the being to produce something of himself in the reality in which he finds himself.

When we enter the third cause of reality we leave the area in which Aristotle concentrated his efforts and enter the area in which Plato concentrated his efforts. It was Plato who emphasized the ideal which all men should strive to attain and which only a few ever attain. Plato stressed the idea of striving to emulate the ideal that all men have in their minds when they are born. Whether men are born with the ideal is besides the point here; the point is that the ideal is that which the being is urged to strive to attain or produce in himself. This is what the third cause is trying to accomplish in the being and in the reality.

FRUITION RELATED TO MOTION

The first cause, we have seen, is related to the material and the second cause is related to the form, so in this cause the fruition is related to motion. After the chaos of the first cause and the stableness of the second cause we have entered the dynamics of the third cause and the emphasis is on the motion towards the production of things.

In the first cause we were concerned with the substrate out of which a becoming took place. Then, in the second cause, we were interested in the substance and its development in our realm of reality. Now what we will be interested in is the specific *illuminated* ideal which the being is asked to strive to accomplish in himself. For man, this illuminated ideal is that which is produced by the writers and thinkers of the age. The new ideals began to present themselves in the history of Western Civilization during the age of the Renaissance and have continued down to the present day. Thinkers and writers have proposed new ideals which man in society should strive to attain.

In our present society we have the American Dream. In Russia there is the Russian Ideal of the society eventually doing away with government and all people living together and helping each other with no need for governments and schools and religions. China offers the same picture of a people striving after some ideal presented by the head of the state. This ideal is often termed ideology, but regardless as to what it is called and in what nation one is living, the object is the same—the showing to the people some ideal toward which to work or strive. This enables the people to start producing and bearing fruits in the reality. The ideologies or the utopian ideals of the writers are those which are specifically illuminated to the being.

When we mention utopian ideas it should be kept in mind that such ideas did not begin with Sir Thomas More;

nor did they begin with Plato and his Republic. In all ages and in all times the third cause of reality has presented some ideal towards which the society is asked to strive. In biblical times there were many works which can be called utopian, and we have the Bible itself as an example of ancient, illuminated, idealist writing. We also have the well known writings of Plato which illuminate the ideal state which men should try to emulate. Beginning with Western Civilization's entry into the third cause around 1500 A.D. we have the first writings about the ideal state and ideal towards which men should strive. This whole area of utopian writings is nothing other than the illuminated ideal which the society consciously or unconsciously strives to emulate. Not much credit is given to the writers who illuminate the ideal which the society eventually strives to emulate; this is an area in which more attention should be paid, for this is what society tries to produce in the third cause. People have made the observation that if one wishes to know what will happen in the next fifty years, one should look at the utopian writers of yesterday. A good present-day example of this illuminated ideal is that of the writings of Karl Marx. This writer illuminated or specified how a society should operate and his ideas and ideals have been adopted by a large majority of mankind.

This is a good place to take note of the fact that the two great Greek thinkers, Aristotle and Plato, have never supplanted one another. There are those who favor Aristotle and those who favor Plato, and neither has convinced the other that their side is the more correct view of reality. The fact of the matter is that neither side can persuade the other because each view includes causes not included by the other view. Aristotle places the emphasis upon the first two causes while Plato places the emphasis upon the last two. Naturally, each has something definite and different to say about reality because each concerns himself with different causes.

We have certainly seen that when nations or societies embrace an illuminated ideal a great amount of energy is let loose producing many new things which were not present in the society before. The Reformation brings to mind the new things that were introduced when a segment of the society entered upon the third cause of reality. We also have the example of the French Revolution, and recently we have the Russian and the Chinese adopting the illuminated ideal.

VALUES AND FRUITFULNESS

We have seen that the first cause was interested in the material ingredients for the becoming of something. In the second cause we were introduced to the principles which were responsible for the development of the being and now we will meet the values which the individual embraces so that he can better bring forth some of the illuminated fruit that is specified by the ideals presented through the society.

The values place responsibility upon the individual. These values are presented so that the individual will develop his singularity and his uniqueness, so that he will develop his relationships with the reality in which he finds himself and so that he will develop the fullness of his person.

In the first cause we are concerned with the major ingredients bringing forth some one new thing. In the second cause we are concerned with the principles developing the one thing, identifying the thing and completing or specifying the thing. From the general of the first cause to the specific of the second cause we now enter the domain of the individual in the third. The purpose of the values is to develop the singularity of the thing, to develop the relationships of the thing and to develop the fullness of the thing. When the values are expressed the emphasis switches from the being of reality to the individual in reality and so we have the desire for the "rights" of the individual man, the God-given rights which no power on earth can take away—government, schools or religions. So the emphasis is now upon the individual and his uniqueness. The relationships of the individual are brought into question and the rights of authority and the dictates of the individual consciousness are a factor to be taken into consideration. The individual no longer is content to complete himself in the operation of the society but desires to fullfill himself by engaging in producing something in the reality from himself.

The three values of *uniqueness, relationship* and *fullness* motivate a being to bring forth the products of his being. When a being places value upon his uniqueness he assumes the responsibility for its singularity and thus the motivation towards a responsible attitude to the self and to other beings. When one places some value upon the uniqueness of his being he automatically assumes some of the responsibility for his actions and so begins the period when he strives to bring forth the fruits of his being. Valuing the singularity of its being produces in the being the desire to bring forth some material goods from its own being and so begins the rise of the industrial age in the society, the age which places the emphasis upon the material products produced by the individual. Ultimately the material products are reduced to the making or the producing of money.

The three values are also based upon the three major ingredients of matter, form and motion. The value of uniqueness is based upon matter while the value of relationship is based upon form and the value of fullness is based upon motion. The object of the value of uniqueness or singularity is the production of some new material from the being. The object of the value of relationships is to produce some new relationships with the being and its reality. The object of the fullness is to allow the being the full measure of happiness which this value motivates the being to achieve.

The value which motivates a being towards relationships with other beings allows for more production or more efficiency in the singular being. This is more aptly said through the cliché, it is not what you know but who you know that brings forth results. This saying is most true because the what a being knows belongs in the second or

62

categorical realm of reality and who you know (relationship) belongs in the third or fruitional realm of reality.

A good example of this value of relationships can be seen in the historical setting of the industrial revolution. When the society changed over from the second cause to the third, there was a gradual coming together of people for the purpose of producing new products. This developed into the factory system that the world has come to know. The production of products before the advent of this system was carried on by the individual person in his little shop or home and consequently the production of products was limited. With the emphasis placed upon the fruition of the society, there was a gradual bringing together of people so that a greater production of goods could be accomplished. This is what the value of relationship accomplishes—more and greater production of goods and a greater efficiency of the individual being.

An example which is common to our day and age is that of the great farming countries of Russia and China. The historical setting is that in which these two great countries were somewhat removed from Western Civilization and when the West entered the third cause and gradually increased the emphasis upon the third cause, these two nations were still emphasising the second cause in Russia and the fourth cause in China. The second and the fourth causes place emphasis upon the stability and harmony of reality and so these societies were devoting their efforts to farming and not towards the production of things. Coming in contact with the dynamic West produced a vast change in these countries and they have now shifted the emphasis to the third cause. We thus see the rise in productiveness of the peoples when they bring together the peoples from the farm and place them in closer contact with each other so that more efficiency and more products can be produced to stay in competition with the West. That is why these countries have undergone so vast a change in the last fifty years or so. Russia has tried to change from a society based upon the second cause and China has and is trying to change their society based upon the fourth cause to that of the third cause. In the West this change was gradual but for these countries they are trying to accomplish in a few years what took the West generations and centuries.

Communism is basically one of the various utopian ideals illuminated before the society, which motivates the society towards the production or fruition of itself. What communism does in the present age is to introduce the third cause to those countries that are viewing reality from causes other than the third cause. Whether the society is in the tribal or first cause or in the developing second cause or in the finalized fourth cause, the purpose of communism is to introduce the third cause to that society. The West was supplied with a great number of utopian writers beginning with Sir Thomas More and it was these writers who brought forth the ideals and illuminated the ideals in their writings, which gave motivation to the society gradually being introduced to the third cause. Communism was and is only one of many motivational and utopian writings produced by the West and so naturally it would not gain any permanent followers of a magnitude of that achieved by having only one illuminated system. When other nations began to try to catch up or adopt the third cause they adopted the utopian writing of the day flourishing in the West and that was Communism, which was basically against the productive system of the time. Countries which hated the West but were also trying to compete with the West naturally adopted the system which proclaimed hatred to the rulers of the productive system of the time (the capitalists), but yet also gave forth illuminated ideals so that production of goods could be achieved by societies without the capitalist overlords which these other countries hated. This is what is even now proclaimed by the followers of the communist ideals—hatred of the capitalist overlords and emphasis upon the production of goods by the society.

THE VALUE OF FULLNESS

We have seen that by placing a value upon the singular being there is placed on the being a responsibility to produce some material goods, usually in the form of money. To achieve a greater amount of effectiveness in the production of things relationships are stressed so that more products can be produced by the individual being, and now finally the motivational value of fullness is expressed. This value motivates the being to achieve a measure of fullness or happiness. Moving oneself towards the full production of your being is the desired value expressed in the third cause. Are you achieving the fullest of your being? is the question often asked of the being who produces the material goods and who has many relationships in the society so that he is more efficient. The ultimate question asked of this productive person is if he is attaining the full measure of his being—is he happily fulfilled? The fullness of one's being is that in which the being achieves in some measure all that he is capable of producing. This value motivates to produce of himself more, so that he will achieve a greater amount of happiness.

Aristotle divided the four causes into two groups. The intrinsic causes were considered to be first two causes. The extrinsic causes were considered to be the last two causes. This distinction is easily made, for one can see that the first cause is concerned with the becoming of the thing and that the second cause is concerned with the development of this thing which had become. It can be seen that the last two causes are concerned with the fruits produced by the thing and the final realization of the thing with the reality in which it finds itself; these last two causes are concerned with the thing and its connection with the reality in which it is connected, and the first two causes are more concerned with the thing itself.

This distinction between the intrinsic and the extrinsic is really an artificial one because in the last analysis all four causes deal in some manner with that which is intrinsic and that which is extrinsic to the thing. In the becoming, the concern of the first cause is in bringing forth something new, but this does not happen in a vacuum. In the second cause the development of the thing is the concern, but this does not take place in a reality devoid of time and history. So, in the third cause, the emphasis is upon the fruits produced by the thing, but this does not take place without the interior motivation of the individual thing which is given an illuminated ideal to strive to attain. In the last cause, which is concerned with the connection of the thing with the reality, this realization can not come about without a goal presented to the thing which the thing should strive to realize. Each cause is really concerned with the individual thing but in different ways, and when distinctions are made between the intrinsic and the extrinsic, this only sets up an unnecessary barrier between the four causes where none really exist and does nothing but confuse the issue and understanding of the causes.

This cause is just as much interested in the thing as the second cause, but it is interested in the thing in a different way than the first and the second cause. It is interested in enabling the thing to bring forth fruits from itself, and to accomplish this it introduces the general ideal, which is specifically illuminated by the society; then the individual through the value placed upon his uniqueness or singularity assumes the responsibility of bringing forth some material goods. To increase the fruition of the thing the value of the relationship between the thing and reality begins to take on greater importance because greater fruition can be achieved in the individual through relationships with other beings. Finally, the thing is motivated by the desire to achieve some measure of happiness or fullness.

We have seen that the first cause is concerned with the general becoming of something. In the second cause we were interested in the specific development of the thing that had become. Now, in the third cause, the emphasis is placed upon the individual thing and the values which motivate the thing to give forth its fruits. The personality is the fruits produced by the individual thing, and so we must consider what personality means.

PERSONALIZATION

Personality allows variety to be produced in the individual thing. The first cause is similar to the seed that is in the ground undergoing development and developing roots and a foundation. The second cause is the actual plant with its definite shape and operation and its definite specie. The third cause is the plumage or the fruits or flowers that the plant produces. It is the variety of fruits and flowers that give variety to the nature of the thing.

The type of personality that is to develop is determined by the second cause. This determination is achieved through the time that a being is born into the reality. Time parcels out a certain measure of motion or a certain variety of fruit or the variety of personalities.

We have pointed out that each cause produces a certain effect and each cause requires a certain kind of energy to produce its effect. A person or being born into reality acquires the kind of energy that enables the particular cause of the time to achieve its effect. The kind of energy needed to achieve the effect of the first cause is different from the kind of energy needed to achieve the second and so on. We know from our own experience that there are four seasons of the year and that history and reality go through cycles in which one period follows another, and we somehow know that people born in a certain period of the year have a different personality than people born in another period of the year. There is a reason for this and it is this: when we enter reality we are motivated or energized by the type of motion which is individuating reality at the time. As we have said, there are four causes representing four periods; consequently there are four basic personalities which will be energized. Each basic personality takes on the characteristics of the motion prevailing at the time when the being entered the reality.

PARTS OF A PERSONALITY

Personalities are, as we said, divided into four groups determined by the cause prevailing at the time the being came into the reality. Besides this, there are the nine categories which will develop or determine the personality. There are seven intensities of motion which individuate the personality. We are back to our three major ingredients, only in different dresses.

Each cause produces a certain effect, and the predominant necessity of the first cause is the practical material that brings about a becoming. This becoming is developed through the nine categories, and the intensity of motion needed is that of courage. Courage is necessary to bring forth something new into reality.

The basic trait of the second cause is that of the dynamic personality. This is the personality which is concerned with the bursting forth into reality of the new one thing which is now going to be developed through the nine categories, and the intensity of motion needed to bring this about is that of confidence and productivity. This is the personality which will begin the effectual development of the second cause.

The basic personality of the third cause is that of the flexible person or being. This being is concerned with the fruitification of the reality and to bring this about all avenues must be open towards the flowering of the being. This cause is also developed through the nine categories of the personality, and the intensity of motion needed to bring this about is that of ingenuity and adaptability. This personality enables all the various and possible fruits and flowers to come forth from the society in which it is found.

The fourth cause is concerned with a basic personality of a thinking person. This personality is concerned with the realization or the finalization of the society or of the thing itself and this personality is also developed through the nine categories of personality. The type of motion needed by this personality to bring about the finalization of the reality presented is that of intensity and poise. This intensity of motion allows the personality to penetrate all facets of the being presented, and poise allows the personality to harmonize all the parts of the reality into one wholeness.

The Greeks placed the four personalities into four material classifications: PRACTICALITY was the EARTH. DYNAMISM was FIRE. FLEXIBILITY was WATER. THINKING was AIR. So we see that in the very beginning of human classification the first classification of personality begins with the material ingredients. This classification is just as good today as the day it was first devised because it is based upon the first cause, the material ingredients for anything.

The second part of the personality is also based upon the second cause and this concerns the categories of development of the being. The nine categories of determination are: 1. determination, 2. stability, 3. activity (our old friends, quantity, quality, relationship), 4. ambition, 5. versatility, 6. sagacity (activity, receptivity and time), 7. perseverance, 8. persistence, 9. initiative (our categories of habits, place and circumstances).

The seven qualities or frequencies of motion are the seven ways in which motion is applied to bring about the individuality of the personality. Courage, confidence, productivity, ingenuity, adaptability, intensity and poise are the seven ways in which motion is applied so that the personalities can accomplish their achievement or effect.

For a better illustration of the four causes working in the determination of the personality, we can take the total year and divide this into four basic parts. Each part represents one basic personality group devoted to the development of that particular cause. Because each cause is developed through the nine categories, there will be nine personalities in the first cause, nine in the second, and so forth. Because the year is divided into four parts, with three months in each part, the nine categories will be spaced in ten-day intervals. Each personality in the group is then spaced through a ten-day period. This enables a new personality to emerge every ten days. So the total personalities in any group of beings amounts to thirty-six. These personalities can be listed as such:

FIRST CAUSE	MATERIAL	CATEGORY	FREQUENCY
Early January	Practicality	Determination	Courage
Mid "	Practicality	Stability	Confidence
Late "	Thinking	Activity	Productivity
Early February	Thinking	Ambition	Ingenuity
Mid "	Thinking	Versatility	Adaptability
Late "	Flexibility	Sagacity	Intensity
Early March	Flexibility	Perseverance	Poise
Mid "	Flexibility	Persistence	Courage
Late "	Dynamism	Initiative	Courage
Early April	Dynamism	Determination	Confidence
Mid "	Dynamism	Stability	Productivity
Late "	Practicality	Activity	Ingenuity
Early May	Practicality	Ambition	Adaptability
Mid "	Practicality	Versatility	Intensity
Late "	Thinking	Sagacity	Poise
Early June	Thinking	Perseverance	Courage
Mid "	Thinking	Persistence	Confidence
Late "	Flexibility	Initiative	Productivity
Early July	Flexibility	Determination	Ingenuity
Mid "	Flexibility	Stability	Adaptability
Late "	Dynamism	Activity	Intensity
Early August	Dynamism	Ambition	Poise
Mid "	Dynamism	Versatility	Courage
Late "	Practicality	Sagacity	Confidence
Early September	Practicality	Perseverance	Productivity
Mid "	Practicality	Persistence	Ingenuity
Late "	Thinking	Initiative	Adaptability
Early October	Thinking	Determination	Intensity
Mid "	Thinking	Stability	Poise
Late "	Flexibility	Activity	Courage
Early November	Flexibility	Ambition	Confidence
Mid "	Flexibility	Versatility	Productivity
Late "	Dynamism	Sagacity	Ingenuity
Early December	Dynamism	Perseverance	Adaptability
Mid "	Dynamism	Persistence	Intensity
Late "	Practicality	Initiative	Poise

We have listed all the traits of personality, showing how each of the traits are related to a given cause and why it is necessary to have nine personalities in each cause; for this

70

represents the nine categories of development of the cause. At the beginning of each cause the presiding basic trait begins the development of the cause. Practicality for the first cause; dynamism for the second; flexibility for the third; and thinking for the fourth cause. We see that the categories are through which the causes develop and in the frequency of motion we see the seven ways in which motion is emphasized so that the right kind of motion can be brought to bear by the given personality. Thus, courage is needed above all else to bring forth some new becoming when there was none before. Confidence and productivity are needed so that the being can be developed to its fullest extent. Ingenuity and stability are the most important ways of emphasizing motion in the third cause, for the greatest fruition is desired. In the fourth cause, intensity is required to bring together all the various manifestations of the reality into finalization. To accomplish this in an agreeable manner, poise is necessary to bring all the factions together.

So we see that the personality is related to the period of reality one is born into. The period determines the material that is to be emphasized and developed through the nine categories and individually completed through the seven frequencies of motion.

There are a great number of books explaining the value of one's birth date in relation to one's personality, and each book more or less is based upon the same empirical fact that the time a being enters reality determines what kind of personality the being will possess. The understanding of causes shown in this work enables one to appreciate that in this, or any reality in which a being finds itself, nothing is left to change. All things fall into a well-conceived and well-executed design. A being is given the personality necessary, at the time the being enters this world or any world, to the reality at the time.

SUMMATION OF THE THIRD CAUSE

In this cause we have considered reality from the viewpoint of producing something from itself. The first cause considers a general becoming; the second cause considers a specific development, and now in this cause we are concerned with the individual and what he produces in himself and for himself.

We have shown that the individual is motivated by some ideal which is specifically illuminated by the reality in which he finds himself. These ideas enable the individual to strive to produce in himself the illuminated ideals favored by the reality.

We have shown that when the individual values his singularity he begins to assume the responsibility which enables him to bring forth the fruits from his own being or self. Relations allow the being to increase his efficiency and fruitfulness, and the value of achieving happiness motivates the individual to accomplish something of his self.

We have also shown that the four causes are to be found in the personality development of the self. The basic material ingredient is based on the first cause. The personality is developed through the categories of development found in the second cause. The intensity or frequency of motion is based upon the third cause.

We have covered three causes so far and are now to enter the fourth cause, which will be concerned with the finalization or the realization of the thing. It should be obvious to all that nothing in reality develops through chance. The old saying from the Bible rings true here, that nothing, not even a hair on a person's head, is left out of the design and development of reality.

IV. THE FOURTH PRESENTATION
OF REALITY

After a becoming is completed and the reality is presented with a new one thing, we are finished with the first cause and enter the second. After the second cause develops the one thing and a developed oneness, identity and completeness is presented to the reality, the second cause is no longer needed and the third cause is called upon to produce the fruits from the thing. After the thing has produced from itself the flowers and fruits of its being, the third cause is completed and the fourth cause is introduced so that the full realization of the thing can take place.

The thing now begins to finalize itself with the reality in which it is participating. The emphasis now shifts from the motivation of the individual thing to the practical realization of the thing with the reality.

We have seen that the general overall consideration of the first cause was the potentiality of a thing. In the second cause the general overall consideration was the actualization of the thing presented through the first cause. In the third cause the general overall consideration was the idealization of the individual thing so that the thing would have some ideal towards which to motivate itself and bring forth fruits. Now, in the fourth cause, the general overall consideration is the finalization or realization of the thing with the whole reality. This means bringing the thing into a harmony with the whole of reality. It means fitting the individual thing into the rhythm and pulse beat of the total reality. The emphasis now shifts from the fruits of an individual thing to the harmony and the working together of all things in the total reality. The consideration shifts from the wants and the desires of an individual to the working together of a whole body of individuals or beings in the reality. This is the general goal of the fourth cause.

We have seen that in each cause there is a class of parts which make up the total cause. We have seen that there are four classes of parts in each cause. Each class pertains to a certain area of consideration in the cause. The four parts for all the causes are the UNIVERSAL; the GENERAL; the SPECIFIC; and the INDIVIDUAL.

In the first cause the universal was the entity; the general the potential; the specific the substrate; and the individual the matter, form and motion.

In the second cause the four parts are the universal being; the general actuality; the specific substance; and the individual essence, existence and operation.

In the third cause the four parts are the universal fruition; the general idealization; the specific illuminated ideal; and the individual singularity, relationships and fullness.

Now, in the fourth cause, the four parts are the universal purpose or goal; the general finalization or realization; the specific substantialization of the reality; and the individual oneness, unity and wholeness.

It can be seen that each cause is related to the other causes in its number of parts and the function of the parts; that is, some parts refer to the universal, some to the general, and so forth. That is why each cause expresses a particular and distinct view of reality, a total view of reality. For this reason, someone looking at reality through one cause will be able to express his reality totally. Someone else looking at reality from another cause will also be able to express his reality totally. This is how the saying about the four corners of the earth developed. The world looks through the four causes when it views reality and at any given time there will be four views of reality presented by mankind. We shall see how this presents itself in the historical section of this work; for the present it is necessary to know that each cause in itself presents a total picture because it has all the parts to present the total picture. Each cause has something to say about the universal, the general, the specific and the individual. A totality is thus presented.

We have said that the universal consideration of the fourth cause is the finalization of a thing with the reality. The general consideration is the harmonization of the thing so that it fits into the reality in a manner that fits the rhythm of the thing with the rhythm of the reality. And the specific consideration is the substantialization of the substance which we have been following through the causes.

Finally, the individual consideration of the fourth cause concerns the oneness of the thing with the reality; the unity of the thing with the reality; and the wholeness of the thing with the reality.

THE TERM ONENESS

The term Oneness can be considered in four different ways, and naturally each way corresponds to a different cause. As we have mentioned before, the final cause is concerned with goals. The final cause is represented in each of the causes because there are goals in each of the causes and these are called the effect of the causes. We have said that in the final cause the goals to consider are the oneness of the thing with the reality; the unity of the thing with the reality and the wholeness of the thing with the reality. So the goals are the oneness, unity and wholeness of the thing. In the other causes these goals are also present but they are expressed in a different manner.

So we have oneness and the other two goals expressed in the first cause in a definite and precise manner, referring to something that only concerns the first cause. Oneness and the other goals are also expressed in the other causes but in another way.

The goal of one appears in the second cause applying to

this "one" presented being. The essence presents a new "one" which is to be developed. This is the actual "one" which the essence will develop into the fully developed "one" through the categories of the second cause. This oneness again pertains to something precise and distinct and is found only in the second cause. It has nothing to do with the oneness of the first cause or any other cause.

The oneness that appears in the third cause applies to the singularity or the uniqueness of the thing. This oneness considers the individual as a unique thing separate and apart from all the other individual things. This oneness begins placing some responsibility upon the individual thing to begin the fruition or the production of the thing. This oneness is also something precise and definite and refers to something only found in the third cause of reality.

ONENESS IN THE FOURTH CAUSE

This oneness considers the complete being or the realized being in relation to itself and with the rest of reality. It is concerned with the harmony of the thing with the rest of reality in which the realized thing should become a one with the rest of the reality. This oneness considers the coming together of the thing with the rhythm and the cycles of the reality in which it finds itself. It considers the coming together of the thing with the rest of reality, so that there will be not a reality of many individual things but a reality in which all are "one."

We already have considered the term unity with regards to the first cause but to go over it once more we say that this unity is something precise and definite. It refers to the coming together of the three major parts so that something becoming united enables a new "one" thing to come into reality.

Unity in the second cause is considering the identity of the new thing. This identity is developed by the thing uniting with the reality in which it is presented, and this uniting allows an identity to be formed with the thing and with the reality. This can readily be seen in our own society when there is such a lack of communication and one hears so much about the search for identity. This is simply the cause or the effect of a lack of unity of the thing with the society. Naturally, this effects those beings which are in the developing cause of reality, that is, the second cause. These beings are the young people and even the older people who for one reason or another are not able to become united with the reality in which they find themselves. They are not able to communicate with this reality and so they are in search of something to communicate with. The result is that they find and form their own sub-societies in which they are able to unite themselves with and thus form some identity. This is the unity that is the concern of the second cause.

In the third cause, the efficient cause, unity is concerned with uniting the thing with other things in the reality so more and greater fruits can come forth from the thing. If the thing was left all to itself and had to produce only from itself, it would not be able to achieve the efficiency as it would if it became united or related to other beings. The larger the relationships that the being achieves, the greater will be the efficiency of the thing in producing fruits from itself. This cooperative unity is designed to achieve or accomplish the maximum production of the being. In human society this is observed through the organizations formed by man to produce a greater amount of benefits and productivity. The industrial factory, the office, the trade unions, the farmer cooperatives, the social and the fraternal organizations all produce for the individual man a greater amount of fruition than the individual would accomplish if left to his own resources.

The unity in the fourth cause considers the thing as a completed reality in which it is united in itself and with the reality in which the being finds itself, and also with the reality that is not experienced. This is a practical unity which is concerned with bringing together all the loose ends of the reality and uniting them. In our reality this would be the harmonization of the society into a unity of the diverse elements, the minority groups and the other various facets that make up a given society.

In all societies this unity can best be understood through the individual holy man who, after a long life of religious devotion, achieves a reality beyond the realm of the experienced reality. This would be the ultimate unity of the fourth cause, achieved by the very few; it is the ultimate example of the unity of the thing with the whole reality, seen and unseen.

Examples of this unity can be seen from the history of the Chinese people. Their thinkers and leaders have expressed the view of unity of the people with the rhythm and harmony of the total reality and this has been their guiding goal through the ages. Their whole history has been the desire to unite themselves with the past through honoring their ancestors; by following the wishes of the parents present harmony is observed and by honoring the aged future harmony is also kept. This is the practical application of the last cause with emphasis upon unification of the thing with the total reality.

So we have seen the four uses of the term unity. In the becoming we were concerned with uniting the thing with the reality so that some identity can be formed. In the third cause we were concerned with the uniting with other things in the reality to form relationships of which more could be achieved by the individual than if he were left alone. Lastly, the fourth cause was concerned with unity of the thing to the rest of reality so that the thing will be in harmony and rhythm with the reality. There is an example of each of these causes being worked out in human society as we shall see in the historical section of this work.

THIRD GOAL OF THE FOURTH CAUSE

The third goal of the fourth cause is the wholeness of the reality. The first goal considers the oneness of the reality, the second goal considers the unity of the reality and now the third goal considers the wholeness of the reality. On the surface the goals may seem similar but they are separate and distinct goals. There can be one reality but not necessarily a united reality or a whole reality. A society can have one nation but it is not necessarily a united society or a society which embraces the whole of the people. In reality such is more often the case than achieving the three goals in one group of people; there are more societies which have one geographical nation but no unity or wholeness than are there societies with three goals accomplished. The geographical oneness has nothing to do with the unity of all the elements in the society nor does it have anything to do with the inclusion of all the parts of the society into one harmonious whole.

The wholeness of the fourth cause can also be considered in four separate and distinct ways. The wholeness is a goal which is to be effected in all the causes.

WHOLENESS OF THE BECOMING

The wholeness of the becoming considers the interrelating of the three major ingredients into a whole. The whole which is produced in the becoming leaves nothing to be desired in the new thing. The thing is not lacking in anything to fully complete the other three causes. In the becoming of a living thing, all the three ingredients are present in the thing itself and this allows for the becoming of a whole, which eventually will be a substance. In a non-living thing motion is outside of the thing and it must rely upon motion coming from the outside; this is why it is called an artificial or inanimate thing and it really is an artificial whole. Motion is not in the thing as a major ingredient; if taken away, the thing is no longer a whole. To be a whole the thing must have the three major ingredients of matter, form and motion working together as a whole to produce the substrate which eventually will bring about the substance. This whole then has reference to the three major ingredients enabling production of a thing which needs

79

nothing from the outside to achieve its purpose. This is the whole of the three major ingredients producing a one substance.

WHOLENESS IN THE SECOND CAUSE

The wholeness that concerns the second cause pertains to the completeness of the being. A being cannot be a whole unless it completes its development by operating in the reality in which it finds itself. Unless the being performs regular actions and has a place in reality and is faced with a definite set of circumstances there is no whole for the being. The being is incapable of completing its development without a definite operation and this is what the wholeness of the second cause tries to achieve. The wholeness of the development of the being in the second cause is simply allowing the being which is developing to have a place and something to perform in the reality in which it finds itself and to be faced with a definite set of circumstances or rules. This enables the being to develop to its fullest extent and the wholeness of the second cause is effected. Strange as this may seem, some societies are lacking in this development. In the United States which places emphasis upon the third cause or production of things, there is often no place for young developing beings and families often do not offer a definite set of rules with which to face reality. The result is that the young people perform no regular meaningful activities in society because there is no place for them in the society and the rules change so often that it is somewhat frustrating to face reality. The result is there are a great number of drop-outs from society of young people who start their own sub-societies or underground societies all because the wholeness of the being is frustrated in its development.

WHOLENESS IN THE THIRD CAUSE

In the third cause wholeness pertains to the fullness of the individual or the happiness which the individual has produced in himself. This wholeness applies to the wholesomeness and the fullness of production achieved through himself and with reality. The ability to fully realize productiveness and to achieve all that is possible is the full measure of happiness that the being is capable of, and this is the wholeness of the third cause.

WHOLENESS IN THE FOURTH CAUSE

The wholeness of the fourth cause refers to the realized thing as part of the harmony of the rest of the reality in which it finds itself and with the total reality both seen and unseen. This is the thing working in unison and rhythm with the whole reality. It is no longer the individual thing considered in itself but the thing belonging to the whole system of realities. In the other three causes the whole more or less pertains to the development of the single being, the whole as it pertains to developing one complete being, and the whole as it pertains to the full production of fruition of itself. Now in the fourth cause the whole pertains not only to the being which is fully realized but to the being which becomes a part of the total reality. This wholeness pertains to the positive contribution that each being offers to the totality of reality. To say that all things in this reality return to nothing is a completely negative approach to reality. Even if something lasts for only a second or two that thing contributed something to the wholeness of reality.

SUMMATION OF THE FOURTH CAUSE

Each cause is considered with the thing and the reality in which the thing finds itself. In becoming something new, the material of the reality in which the becoming takes place supplies the possibility of a new becoming. In the second cause the being relates itself to the development of the self with the reality in which it has its being. In the third cause the thing considers the fruition of the self with the reality which allows the fruits to come forth. In the fourth cause the thing is considered as contributing something to the wholeness or the totality of the complete reality, experienced as well as inexperienced. If we stopped at the third cause we could arrive at the conclusion that the major goal of all things is for the individual being to bring forth the fruits of itself to achieve its total happiness, and that would be the end of it. The fourth cause prevents emphasizing the singular individual but brings out the contribution that all beings make towards the total wholeness of reality. From the smallest and most insignificant atom to the grandest galaxies all participate and contribute to the totality of reality. This is what the fourth cause expresses as the ultimate goal for all things.

Each cause has a definite period in which to work itself out in any given reality and we shall see that in the history of mankind it usually takes about 500 years to work out each cause. When the last cause has been completed this does not mean the termination of the reality, but rather that the full realization of the reality has been achieved. This completed reality then becomes a part of the harmony of the total reality.

THE FOUR CAUSES COVERED INTELLECTUALLY

We have covered the four causes in a more or less purely intellectual manner. To complete the picture let us look back and see the working of the four causes through historical events not only of the Western Civilization but of of the total reality of man.

There is nothing mysterious about all this, for it is simply understanding the patterns through which things move so as to develop to the fullest extent possible, in order that the totality of reality can be achieved. These are not laws by which all things are governed because law implies that a lawgiver has imparted a law to his subjects and the subjects, knowing the law, follow or do not follow it. This has nothing to do with the being or thing knowing the law or not knowing the law or following the law or not following the law. The thing in question may know nothing about the causes which effect his development but through these causes he or it develops whether or not he knows the reasons for it.

Understanding the causes will enable the being to comprehend why new things develop in society at a certain given time and that what once was the accepted manner of looking at reality is no longer observed, a different approach is undertaken by the society or the reality. The explanation is that one cause has developed to the fullest extent possible and has achieved its effect and the newer or the next cause is beginning to exert itself to bring forth its viewpoint upon reality so that further development can be achieved in the reality.

CAUSES IN HISTORY

In this section we wish to show the working of causes in a given reality. A person with a cynical outlook upon reality may say that there is no rhyme or reason why anything takes place and the whole of our reality is just one big accident. There is not much chance of convincing such a person of another view. This work is mainly directed to those people who somehow feel that there is a rhythm and cycle to all things and that reality follows a pattern.

It is not the object of this work to give an opinion about any particular historical events but rather to shown how a pattern occurs in the history of any given group of people and for the whole reality. We shall show that certain changes take place in any given society and that these changes are the result of the causes.

When historians place titles upon ages they do this because the particular age represented a definite view of reality. The Dark Ages, the Middle Ages, and Modern Times are all three different views of reality and they represent three different causes. Because the views that society harbored at one time, and what they tried to accomplish, were so different from other times, a person studying the ages can label the times. This is the result of the working of the causes. We would like to show the causes at work in the overall picture of our reality, then to the particular history of a given group of people. In this way the whole as well as the parts may be understood through the workings of the causes.

THE FIRST CAUSE: THE BECOMING, THE OVERALL PICTURE

We are all familiar with the theories of evolution which say that man and all the other animals went through a process in which the size, shape and intelligence of the beings improved and progressed to the state in which we now observe them. This theory of evolution is perfectly in accord with the first cause of reality, except, like most new theories, it goes a little too far. Evolution applies to a period in our world which is called pre-history. It was the period of becoming for the total world in which we live. All things were in a state of flux and becoming and from the bones and other fragments found, a picture has been drawn of this period with animals and plants going through a process in which they slowly developed and evolved. In this period the whole reality was in the first period of development.

All the species were in the first period of development and that is why some species resemble other species, for all things were in the becoming stage; in each species three major ingredients of matter, form and motion were bringing about eventual development of a specific thing. This period of evolution or becoming is the same period our Western Civilization went through which our historians call the Dark Ages. In the individual person this is the period of becoming which takes place in the mother and in the early ages of life. It is the psychological period of the "id" in which all things are murky and dark with all sorts of things popping into the mind and leaving the mind and everything in flux.

In this period of becoming or evolution which is the first cause of this reality, man as we know him today naturally was not present. He was in a stage of development along

84

with the rest of the reality. So what we find is many varieties of man-like people who can not really be classified as a developed man for the simple reason that mankind at this period was in the stage of becoming or developing into a human being.

THE SECOND CAUSE: THE BEING, THE OVERALL PICTURE

When the period of becoming or evolution finally developed to the point in which a fully developed specific thing was presented to the reality, then the first period passed and the second period entered the history of this world. This second period began the development of the one thing presented through the first cause. We have now presented one human being which must be developed. This development takes place through the categories and that is why we enter the period of the beginning of society or civilization. We enter the formative part of our reality in which societies are founded so that the human person will be able to develop to the greatest capacity possible and this is the reason it is necessary to have societies or civilizations. It is through the categories that the human race is developed and that is what the second cause is all about: the development of the one thing presented through evolution or becoming. This period begins written history, or the formalized history of mankind.

It is interesting to note that each cause has a definite place in our world. It is agreed by almost all people who have studied the subject that man started to evolve or to begin the first cause in the region of Africa or in a place south of the equator. After the period of becoming and when the second stage was entered, the action shifted to North of the equator in the region of the Nile and Egypt of today. This is the place in which the second period begins in world history and this is the region which concentrated upon the development of the being of man.

This is the period in which the biblical narrative begins

and in which all the written history begins for all the societies of mankind.

THE END OF THE SECOND CAUSE:
THE OVERALL PICTURE

The completion of the second cause for all of mankind was at the birth of Christ. This was the fullness of time in which the full development of mankind was accomplished and a full human being was achieved. In this period we have the three major ingredients developed to their fullest. The Roman government represented the full development of the material aspect of this reality. The Greek intellectual achievement was the full development of the cultural development of mankind and the Jewish development was the full development of the spiritual or religious achievement of mankind. These three major ingredients which are necessary for the full development of mankind were fully developed and became one at the time that Christ was born. This is why it was known as the fullness of time for it is the period in which the full development of mankind was achieved and it is the period in which the second cause was completed for the whole of mankind.

We have in this period the full completion of the human government in which laws were devised to embrace the whole of mankind, not considering race or religion. In this period the Greeks achieved the full development of the intellectual or formative development of mankind. Also following this trend in human development was the Jewish religion which was becoming aligned with the Roman government and the Greek cultural development and when the birth of Christ occurred we have the full development or the full identity of mankind achieved. Time as we have seen concerns the establishing of an identity and when there is the fullness of time the full identity of mankind is established and developed.

In the second period of the development of mankind we can find all the forms into which it is possible for a human society to develop. The highest was achieved by the Romans who produced a law which is still used today in all nations of the world except China and Turkey.

The Greeks developed the highest form of plastic arts, plays, theater, paintings, architecture, scientific and philosophical thinking and all the other intellectual attainments that is possible for the human intellect to develop. All that the human mind is capable of upon any subject was developed to the fullest by these people and this was their contribution to the development of mankind in the second cause.

The Jewish people developed the highest form of religious aspirations possible for mankind to achieve and these people brought forth a religion that is possible for the total mankind to adopt and embrace. Incidentally, at the death of Christ the three languages were placed above the cross to exemplify this historical fulfillment in the development of mankind.

We can see the development of the essence, the existence and the operation of mankind through these three groups of people. The overall accomplishment of the Roman government was the establishing of "one" government with "one" set of laws for the whole of mankind.

The Greeks accomplished the unity of all mankind for they developed the existence of mankind so that it was now possible for man to completely identify himself with the totality of reality. The Greeks developed and completed all the manners and ways in which is was possible for mankind to express itself so that it would be possible to achieve the fullest possible identity with the reality in which it finds itself and with the whole of reality.

The Jewish people developed all the ways and manners in which it is possible to operate in this reality and this religion offered a place to all the peoples born into this reality. This religion expressed regular observance of religious duties, regular performance of religious acts, and emphasis upon a place in the scheme of this reality. And the reality that is not experienced allowed the human person to face reality though the set of rules which the religion offers to its members. This instilling into the people habits of regular devotions and performance of repeated acts of devotion, offering a place in the scheme of thing and allowing the people to face reality through a definite set of rules completed the person and also completed the development of the whole of mankind from the overall historical picture.

THE THIRD CAUSE: THE OVERALL PICTURE

We of the Western civilization exemplify the working of the third cause in the totality of mankind. We exemplify the development of the individual and the fruition of mankind. The world has never before seen such production as has come forth from the Western group of mankind. This group has developed and produced all the goods and all the major services the individual is capable of using. The emphasis has been upon the uniqueness of the singular being, the relationships of the being to the rest of reality, and the happiness and the fulness of this being. It is in the West that the efficiency of things and production of things is given the greatest consideration; the emphasis upon values and motivation of the person is given a great amount of consideration by society.

THE FOURTH CAUSE: THE OVERALL PICTURE

The final or the fourth cause has been developed by the Eastern people and they have placed emphasis upon the realization and the finalization of things. The East has emphasized the fourth cause through the ages and this is observed through their thinkers and their leading writers and also their society, for they have placed society as viewing all things in relation to the harmony that is found in reality. The Eastern nations and people view reality through the workings of the fourth cause in which man should be in harmony with this total reality that is presented. The ultimate example of this view is the manner in which some of the holy men of the East go out of their way to avoid harming any and all living creatures. Since they view all things as being a part of the overall whole, the smallest and the most minute thing contributes something to this reality and the smallest thing has just as much right as man for living in this reality.

POLARIZATION OF THE FOUR CAUSES

What we have in effect is the place which the four causes have and work themselves out in this reality. South of the equator in Africa we have the working out of the first cause for from there all things began and started to become. North of the equator around the Mediterranean we have the development of the second cause of this reality in which mankind was developed. This area is where the Romans, Greeks and Jews developed to the fullest the second cause of reality in mankind, this is where the full identity of mankind was accomplished with the birth of Christ.

Moving West we go into the region of the third cause in which the emphasis is upon the fruition of the individual thing and the production of things, and we enter the area of the Western Nations. The United States is an example of the fruition of reality in which fruits and products of all kinds come forth from society as if by magic. The emphasis as we have said is upon the fruition of the individual person and what the individual person can achieve.

Moving further West we enter the area of the fourth cause which is exemplified by the Eastern nations and people. Eastern people, have from the times of their ancient past to the present, have stressed the harmony and the final purpose of mankind. Reality should be lived in conjunction with the rest of the living things and in harmony with the rhythm and the cycles of the total reality. This is the message of the fourth cause and this is the effect which the Eastern peoples have sought.

What we have then in the total world is four causes producing four different views upon reality and each cause is trying to produce a different effect. This is what makes the world such an interesting place in which to live. One area concentrates upon the first cause or the becoming of something. The next area concentrates upon the development of the reality and the third area upon the production and the fruition of the reality, while the fourth places emphasis upon the finalization and the harmonization of the reality with the total reality.

This is the working of the four causes in this reality. This overall picture is given with the intention of showing that each segment of this reality has something different to say concerning reality. One segment is no better than any other although the people living in one area will think that their view of reality is the best of all views. It is the hope of this work to make known that the total reality can have four equally valid views and the four views are the only possible way of understanding the total picture of this reality.

We have briefly covered the general picture of the four causes as they apply to this reality. What we would now like to show is a specific example of the working of the four causes. The best place to go for a specific example of anything is that area in which the second cause developed, around the Mediterranean Sea where the development of mankind took place. We are able to cite examples of the workings of the four causes in the history of people because from this area we have the story of the complete society, the story of a society that has moved through all the causes. Not only do we have the story of one society here but of many societies who have moved through the four causes.

A SPECIFIC PICTURE OF THE WORKING OF THE FOUR CAUSES

We have for our specific study the history of three groups of people, the Romans, the Greeks and the Jewish societies, of the period which covered the fulfillment of the development of mankind in the second stage of reality. The history of each society clearly shows the development of the four causes.

Each society went through a tribal period in which the people formed one society. Each society went through a period in which development took place, the period of their kings and royal families. Each society then went through a period in which the development of the individual and the fruition of the individual was the major consideration of the times and this period lasted the same amount of time as the other two periods, and then the final period was entered into when the reality of the societies were finalized and this is the period which is concerned with the realization of the society.

THE ROMAN HISTORY AND THE FOUR CAUSES

We do not have a historic written record of the beginning of the Roman society. Historians say that the Latins migrated to the regions which were later to become the Roman state before 1000 B.C. If, and we shall see that recorded history bears this out, each cause accomplishes its effect in a society during a 500 year period, we can say with reasonable certainty that the Latins came into the Po valley around 1,500 B.C. It then took these people 500 years to go through a process of becoming which is the concern of the first cause. After the process of becoming took place, the formation of the society began to develop and this was the period of the kings and the monarchy. The development of the curiae, or brotherhoods, for electoral and military purposes took place in this 500 year period, as well as the other social customs of these people.

When the formation of these people were completed and the second cause was accomplished there was a change from the concentration upon the development of the society to one in which the fruits of the society began to be the dominant occupation of the people. Thus we enter the period of the Roman Republic which began with the overthrow of the monarchy in 509 B.C. Thus begins the period of the third cause, which will stress the idealized and the illuminated. This is the period in which the Romans were singled out to start the production of a world state in which all nations and all people could be a part and citizens thereof. Thus begins the production of laws which will be able to embrace the whole of mankind. This foundation of the Roman Republic begins the period in which the fruits of the Roman people will begin to come forth and these fruits eventually will be the establishment of a state in which the whole of mankind will be included. This is the ultimate production and the ultimate legacy of the Roman people and their civilization. The fruits of this civilization came forth for a period of 500 years when the fourth period was entered into, which was the realization of the Roman civilization.

During the period of the third cause, Roman society and law came into contact with all the known societies of the day and this was the period in which they came into contact with the Greeks and the Jewish people and the other peoples of the world. Wars were being waged and treaties were made. When all the peoples were gathered together and all the contacts made with the governable people of the age then the third period was ended and the finalization of the government began. This started with the governing of the empire by Julius Caesar. This was the man who began the finalization of the government and this was the man who began the fourth cause of the Roman society. The finalization of the government took about 500 years to complete. This finalization period was the one in which the government was realized as a completed thing. This completed thing enabled all peoples to be under the protection of one type of law and one form of government and this was the realization of the Roman government. This realization continues to the present day. The realization of something does not mean the termination but rather the completeness of something, and this completeness was achieved during the period of the fourth cause.

GREEK HISTORY AND THE FOUR CAUSES

The Greeks followed the same process in the foundation of their society as did the Romans. There was the period of migration with the coming of the people to the land in which they were to settle; after the society was presented with one body of people there began the period of the second cause. The migration of people took place beginning around 1500 B. C. when Achaeans pushed into northern and central Greece and probably took possession of Crete around 1450 B.C. The foundation of the society for the Greek states begins the period of the first cause and it ends when the being of the society starts to develop. This is the period in which the monarchy begins to develop. It will be seen that a new society occurs when there is a migration of people to some new land. This migration is a sign of the first cause in action for it concerns itself with major material ingredients for the society.

The development of the Greek city states took place in the period of the second cause, from about 1000 B.C. to 500 B.C. This period corresponds to the period in Roman history in which the kings and the monarchy and royalty formed the society into a developed one being which history has given as Greek culture and civilization.

From the period of 500 B.C. to the end of the third cause, which as we have said before was with the birth of Christ, this period was the one in which the production or the fruition of the society took place. In this period the intellectual map of mankind was charted, so to speak. All the categories of the mind were charted by the Greeks and this was their ultimate contribution to the development of mankind. Philosophy, in all its aspects, was mapped so thoroughly that to this day no new areas of consideration have been introduced in this field. Literature in all its areas of consideration was a creation of the Greek mind and in this sphere no new categories have been introduced since the production of the Greeks. Architecture, art and science have been elaborated to the fullest and to this day we use

93

the theories proposed by the Greeks between the years 500 B.C. to 0 B.C. During this time that the expansion of the Greek culture took place the Roman nation was undergoing a similar expansion of their holdings. The period in which all the fruits and flowers of the Greek people came before the world is called the Golden Age of Greece but in reality it was the productive period of the third cause operating in their society.

In the third period Greece came into contact with the Roman and the Jewish contribution to the development of mankind and at the birth of Christ of the fullness of time was accomplished in which mankind received its full identity. The Roman laws were wedded to the Greek intellectual contribution and the Jewish religion was united to the government of all of mankind which resulted in the completion of the second cause for the whole of mankind.

JEWISH HISTORY AND THE FOUR CAUSES

The same thing was happening to the Hebrews as to the Romans and the Greeks and at the same time. Around 1500 B. C. the Hebrews migrated into the land of Egypt and began to become a distinct social organization. Each of these people which we are discussing entered the pages of history beginning with a migration to the land in which they were to become a distinct contribution to the development of mankind. These three peoples are the culmination of the development of the second cause in mankind. There were certainly older cultures and civilizations before these three groups of people. Each of these people entered an area after coming from another place and the area in which they entered was always inhabited by other people, who also had some form of society. It was these groups who entered the history to close the period of the second cause which presented the fullest development of mankind.

The Hebrews then entered the area of the Egyptians and also entered the historic pages of mankind. From 1500 B.C. to 1000 B.C. they also went through their period of becoming in which they were organizing themselves from the tribal state of the first cause. The second period was entered into with the establishment of a kingdom of Israel under the ruler David according to the alloted time schedule of 500 year intervals. David was the king of the Hebrews from 1000 B.C. to 975 B.C. So begins the period in which the formation of the Hebrew civilization is the major objective. The formative period lasts for the same amount of time as the other periods and ends around 500 B.C. when the building of the second Temple begins, around 520-515 B.C.

The fruition of the Hebrews begins as does their relationships with the rest of the known world and they slowly join with the Romans and the Greeks into one developed humanity. In this period we see the Romans becoming the ruling people and the Greek intellectual achievement spreading throughout the world, which was conquered by the Romans. Also in this time the Jewish religion is being spread throughout the world which has been conquered by the Romans and intellectualized by the Greeks.

The fourth period begins with the birth of Christ whose presence represents the fulness of time of mankind or the fulness of identity achieved by the human race.

In the third period there was a coming together of the three major peoples and in the fourth period there was the realization of these three major strains which allowed the full development of mankind to take place. Thus the Jewish religion at the period when it was realized was called a different name from that which was developed during the first three causes and so we have the Christian Religion. Also during this period the Roman government realized its purpose and it was the single world government and the first government to be able to govern the different peoples; this government began its period of realization with the reign of Augustus Caesar. This period also saw the spreading of the Greek culture which all the peoples—under the influence of Rome—were able to digest because it was the second language of the civilization.

The finalization of the development of mankind took place during the next 500 years. In this period the union of the Romans, Greeks and the Christian religion took effect and the completion of this development ends the second cause as it concerns the whole of mankind. This cause has concerned itself with the specification or the formation of the being of mankind. The governmental, intellectual and religious aspirations have been developed in which the whole of mankind could be able to participate and form their society.

THE FOUR CAUSES IN OUR INDIVIDUAL SOCIETY

We have seen that in any period of becoming the first period of the society begins with a migration into something unfamiliar which opens new doors and produces new motives to begin the organization of the society. The primitive people of Northern Europe who were not included in the original Empire of Rome now began a migration into the Empire and slowly assimilated into the Empire and also began to organize their own civilizations patterned after the Roman, Greek and Christian principles which have been instilled in all who have been associated with the Empire.

FIRST PERIOD OF OUR CIVILIZATION

The period of our becoming a major world civilization is called by historians the Dark Ages. This may be an apt name if it is understood in a positive manner. In this period the becoming of the civilization is taking place. All the tribes and all the strong families are forming and becoming a new world society. This period takes about the same amount of time as any other period of the development of mankind, 500 years. So from the period of 500 A.D. to the period of 1000 A.D. we have the emphasis upon the first cause or the becoming of the new society.

Naturally when something new is developing that which was accomplished in the past is overlooked because the peo-

ple have not arrived at the mental stage of understanding
the accomplishments of the past, so naturally many of those
accomplishments will be destroyed or overlooked and will
have to be learned over again.

OUR CIVILIZATION DEVOTED TO THE FRUITION OF MANKIND

Naturally the older civilization will not have accomplished its purpose in vain. What it had accomplished was the formal development of the whole of mankind. All the categories for the full development of mankind were accomplished in the second cause. Now in the next civilization the purpose will be to develop the third cause which will be the fruition of mankind or the production of all the products and all the fruits that mankind is capable of. The first general cause pertaining to the whole of mankind concerns the becoming of the material ingredients and this ultimately concerns the Father of the ultimate trinity. The next cause which concerns the formation of the whole of mnakind concerns the second cause or the Son of the ultimate trinity and this deals with the categorical formation of the being of mankind. So now in the third period we are going to be concerned with the third ultimate ingredient and this is the motion or the spirit of the ultimate trinity. The motion is concerned with the individuation and the fruition of the whole of mankind, which is taking place throughout the world; and this is seen by the numerous countries and nations being formed and the many peoples and societies declaring themselves distinct individuals.

CHURCH HISTORY A GOOD GUIDE TO THE WORKING OF THE CAUSES

The realization of the Hebrew religion called itself Christianity after the person whose birth signaled the beginning of the realization of the Hebrew religion. This new religion was the completion and the realization of Hebrew religion and it was developed under the Greek intellectual culture. When the new civilization began, there also began some conflict with the views of the religion from the eyes of Greek influence. In another sense the new religion which was the realization of the Hebrew was also in its first period which represented the becoming. The people who favored the first or becoming period and also represented the realization of the Jewish religion did not view the new civilization with a pleasant eye. When the becoming of the new society was achieved and the society entered the period of the second cause, there was a split between the factions that represented the first period of the new church and those people who represented the new second cause which was just starting to form a new society. This was the split between the Eastern and the Western Churches which formally occurred, almost 500 years after the becoming started in 1054 A.D. This is a sure sign of the society entering the next period of its development. The Eastern Churches followed the first cause of the new church and represented the becoming period of the new church. Now that the society was entering the second period, the formative period of its development, there would naturally be a split as to which view to look upon reality and this causes the formal separation of the two churches. The Western Church entered the formative period in which its institutions were developed and the emphasis was upon the formal development of the church.

So it is not surprising to find that when the society enters the third period of its development a new viewpoint in the Christian religion will present itself. The second cause represents the formal development of the society. In 1517 Martin Luther began expressing the view of the third cause from the religious point of looking at reality. This is the view expressing the individual and the fruition of the individual person and so there is another break in the Christian Church because another view is presented. The Eastern Church expresses the view of the first cause or the becoming of things; the Catholic Church expresses the view of the formal development or the being of things and this is the second view of reality; the northern or the reformed church as it is called views reality from the third cause expressing the individual and the fruition of the individual.

The next period should see the introduction of the fourth cause in the Christian Church which will represent the finalization of the Christian view upon reality. This view will also represent the Christian religion but it will be viewing reality from the fourth cause which will be different from the Eastern, the Western or the Northern Churches and perhaps can be called the view from the Southern Churches which are yet to come and express themselves.

FOUR CAUSES EXPRESSING THEMSELVES IN POLITICAL LIFE

In the political life of the Western society the four causes are clearly marked. In the first period of the becoming of Western society, this period was called the Dark Ages because nothing presented itself as developed and categorized. During this period the political life of the society was devoted to the becoming of one society. The political structure was that of strong families, tribal chiefs and lesser nobility, and a few strong and courageous leaders who were forming or bringing together the major ingredients which would create a society. This is the period of the strong man with the sword who is courageous enough to brave the unknown so that some becoming can take place. These men are the father of the new civilizations. They are the bold men who do not really know where the society is going but they do know that some becoming should take place. These strong men and their families are slowly coming together through marriage and mutual interests until they will present to the reality one complete governing body for the new society. This governing body is necessary to develop the society in the second cause and it is during this period that the becoming of the political body is being delivered. This political body was presented to reality in the year 962 when Pope John XII crowned Otto, the Saxon King of Germany, as Holy Roman Emperor. This institution was the political body which was to develop the civilization in the second cause. It was never the realized Empire of the Roman civilization because the Roman Empire represented the fourth cause or the finalization of a long political development whereas this Holy Roman Empire was presented to reality for the purpose of developing a new society and not the culmination of one. This Holy Roman Empire was phased out of the picture officially in 1806 but its purpose was actually finished when the second cause was completed around 1500 A.D.

THE SECOND PERIOD IN OUR SOCIETY

With the presentation of a political body began the second cause. Most people know that all the formal institutions of the society were brought to development during the second period of the society. A government which allowed all the people of the society to participate in the conduct of affairs was the feudal system. This system gave a place and a position to all members of the society and allowed a stable platform for the development of the political body. The Christian Church was organized as a formal institution during this period and it is in this period that the Catholic Church feels much at home for it is the period in which the institutional development of the church was achieved. Crusading Orders came into being in this period as well as the Begging Orders such as the Franciscan, founded by Francis of Assisi (1182-1226), and the Dominican Order founded by Dominic (1170-1221). These Church organizations formed and developed the society so that the people would have a love for all members of the society however how low his estate in life, and they instructed society in the beliefs and understanding of their religion.

Having one language for the developing society was a great asset. Because of the small size of the various states and the petty view of the rulers there would be a tendency to stifle development. This was avoided through the use of one language by the learned professions. The doctors, lawyers, teachers, monks, priests were all able to travel from place to place and to converse in one language with members of the same and like professions and thus the full development of the society was accomplished. The second cause is most concerned with the development of the categories for it is through the categories that something develops and it is the learned professions which bring forward the various categories through which the society will develop.

SCHOLASTICISM: THE INTELLECTUAL DEVELOPMENT

The intellectual development of the society was accomplished through the institution called scholasticism. Besides a single system of government being formed and the formal institutions of the church developed, intellectual institutions also were developed and presented in this period. Theology and philosophy were developed and naturally Aristotle would be of absorbing interest to the thinkers of the second period for this Greek thinker concentrated his efforts upon the first and second period which emphasized the categories and the formal development of reality. So this school system allowed the formal development of the society through the logical and the rational order, which is the order of the second cause, and this is the foundation of any school system.

In the second period of the society a new form of buildings developed, the Gothic and the Romanesque styles. They were presented to the reality as something original and distinct from any other society.

To sum up the second cause in our society we can say that all the formal development took place in this period. Music, architecture, schools, philosophies and theologies, civil and religious law and the moral practices of governments and society were developed during this period. This was the period of development of the Being of the society after the becoming was effected during the Dark Ages.

THE THIRD CAUSE IN OUR SOCIETY

It was said before that the first cause is devoted to the becoming of anything and this was the concern of the Dark Ages in Western Society. After the Dark Ages, the second cause was entered and this was the concern of the being of society which was called the Middle Ages. The formation and the development of society took place in this era. The third cause places the emphasis upon the fruitional aspects of society. As the Dark Ages were concerned with the potential or the possibility for a new society and as the Middle Ages were concerned with the Actuality of the society, so now in the third cause we will be concerned with the idealization of the reality. The use of the term ideal is meant to be taken in a positive frame of mind for the ideal is necessary for the fruition of the thing.

With the shift to the third cause, the emphasis is upon the individual and the fruition of the individual. There is a renewed interest in the classical literature of Roman and Greek society. The emphasis is upon the humanities with the glorification of the individual and at the same time the glories of antiquity take on the glow of being the ideal place in which to live and conduct the affairs of life. The search for the ideal was now the general emphasis of the society. This search led men to begin the exploration of the world and to begin to become related with the whole of the world so that the individual could fulfill himself to the greatest possible extent. This search for the ideal led men to study the literature and writings of the ancients and the thought was that the ideal was already achieved by this society. Other men such as Sir Thomas More wrote books of a mystical land in which the ideal society was perfected where all men lived in perfect accord with each other.

With the writing of More's book *Utopia* the reign of

Aristotle ended and the reign of Plato began. Society in the third cause will be concentrating upon the fulfillment of the individual and the betterment and progress of society. There will be presented in an ever increasing measure a long line of writers who will offer the illuminated ideal to society so that society will strive to produce something of itself and bring forth the new society. For the ideal is that which should be produced in society. It is the ideal which motivates society to produce something and to get society moving.

Idealism is to be found in all segments of reality and in all times but the third cause places the emphasis upon the ideal; that is why so many writers of the ideal society come forth during the third cause. Using Sir Thomas More as a starting point (1478-1535) we can name a group of writers who are concerned with the ideal situation for man. Rousseau (1712-1778) proclaimed the ideal period of mankind was the natural state of man when no artificial forms or institutions hamper the freedom of man. Karl Marx (1818-83) proclaimed that if all men were instructed in a proper fashion there would be no need for governments and men would live happily together without the constrictions of state, schools or religious institutions. The ideal was embraced in philosophy by such thinkers as Descartes (1596-1650) who best summed it up by his statement, "I think, therefore I am." Thinking concerns itself with the ideas or the ideal and according to those who embrace the third cause, the ideal is sufficient to guarantee one's reality. Idealism brought forth the Romanism in paintings often referred to as the impressionists. Jean-Jacques Rousseau (1712-1778) was the outstanding forerunner of romanticism who placed final authority on the powers of intuition; he gave each man personal sovereignty in matters of thought and thus every man was able to view reality wholly through the ideas that each obtained within himself.

It should not be surprising that in all facets of reality which are viewed from the third cause, each facet will depend largely upon the general idealism prevailing in the reality. Whether it be in theology or religion—we have the protestants or the reformers and the more appropriate word would be the individualistic Christian Churches. In philosophy we have the idealistic thinkers beginning as far back as Sir Thomas More and continuing to the present and latest thinker who has an ideal program for the betterment of the world. In science we have a program in which ideas and ideals are used to bring forth new products. It will be noted that when every new product is presented to the reality there is someone who will say that this is the ideal product to end all wars, end romantic problems, improve the human condition and in general improve the total lot of mankind. The production of products goes along with the same idealistic thinking and it is necessary that this be so because without idealism it would be impossible to motivate individuals to produce and bear fruit.

We have lived in the period of idealism for about 500 years and so this period is slowly drawing to an end and the next period or the fourth cause will be presenting itself. As a matter of fact the fourth cause is presenting itself in our period of time. The working of the four causes can be seen in the area of production. In the beginning the productive industry was owned and operated by the capitalists or those who had an idealistic conception of money. The beginning of the productive industry was chaotic as any beginning is; the next phase was that in which industry began to be developed and the particular industry began to find all the roads towards which it could develop. Then the productive phase came along and emphasis was upon the efficiency of production. We are now seeing the beginning of the fourth phase in which the industries merge with one another so that there will be a harmony among the productive industries and a finalization and realization. This is the natural and progressive way the causes work in any given situation.

We see that a great many industries and a great many unions are thinking of merging with one another and this is a sign of the workings of the fourth cause. So the third cause is coming to an end and the fourth cause is beginning to exert itself in our society. There are many signs being presented that this is the situation. On the political scene the United States, which represents the third cause, is drawing closer and closer to the society which best exemplifies the fourth cause, the Chinese, and in time the Chinese influence will become more predominant as the world turns to the fourth cause.

THE FOURTH CAUSE IN OUR HISTORY

In the fourth cause the key word is "Merge." It can be said that the key word in the first cause is "Becoming"; the key word in the second cause is "Forming" and the key word in the third cause is "Producing."

We have noted before that a given area of this world places a certain emphasis upon one cause to the exclusion of the others. The tribes and clans place the emphasis upon the first cause. The European scene shows the emphasis upon the second cause with the emphasis upon the formal structure of reality. In the United States emphasis upon the third cause or the productive and efficient is well known. Since the European man has not entered the fourth phase of reality as of yet, the cause can best be seen from the eyes of the Chinese culture and viewpoint. The Chinese view reality with the idea of merging with the natural world and with the supernatural in which all will be of one harmony and one complete whole. The emphasis is not upon the individual but upon the individual and the society merging into one reality. This is the emphasis not only of China but a great part of Asia as well.

Speaking about world viewpoints we can also speak about world personalities. Each world view has an archetype personality which best exemplifies that world view. We have noted before that there are four basic types of personalities and we have said that each personality is based upon one of the causes. Let us see what is the archetype personality in each world view.

105

DOMINANT PERSONALITIES

The type of personality best suited to bring about a becoming of anything from a chaotic state is one with the courage to face reality, strong enough to control the primitive forces surrounding him. This is the practical type, strong enough to face a world which presents a chaotic state in reality. So begins the reign of Clovis I (466-511) king of the Franks who begins the becoming of the new Western society. The strong man with the sword who is not afraid to start something is the reigning personality in the age which starts a becoming of a new reality from the state of non-reality.

The personality needed to bring about the development of the newly presented being or the newly presented society is one in which the dynamic trait is predominant. The development of something new is always a dynamic event and this is the type of personality that we will see in the Middle Ages: the personality who has confidence and is productive in bringing something new into development. New institutions of government, intellectual and religious, are demanded of the times and this is the personality who best is capable of providing these things for the new society. All the categories of society must be developed.

The third cause demands that something be produced and brought forth from the society and the personality best suited to perform these functions is one who is flexible enough to see the means in which something can come forth. This personality needs to be ingenious and to be adaptable to the circumstances in order to produce something. The flexible personality can see the various means in which it is possible to do something and to produce something. To ingeniously devise something and to adapt it to the times brings forth something from society. This type of personality is best seen in the American or the United States personality. This personality is un-formal. He does not look through the categories of being and he does not concern himself with being. He is concerned with the third cause and not with the formation of anything. He wants to find new markets, devise new products and adapt these products to the circumstances of the times. Technology is the concern of the man looking through the third cause. Money is a flexible tool in which to bring about the production of things. Max Weber (1864-1920) traced the rise of the productive society of capitalism to the rise of influence of the Protestant Reformers and with good reason. These were the men who were representing the third cause and since Europe still represented the second cause, most of the reformers left their native homeland and came to a new land in which they would be able to work out their view of reality. This third view is best seen in the United States.

What is needed in the fourth cause is a personality that is able to think things through and to be able to see all the various manifestations of reality and to merge them into a oneness, unity and a whole. This is the thinker and the realizer. This personality needs to be intense and to penetrate the world around him so that he can see all the traits and all the views in reality and to merge these characteristics into a whole. To accomplish this poise is needed to bring about a merger in a natural or harmonious manner. The Chinese best represent this view of reality. Another thing to keep in mind is the historical fact that China was and is ruled by Mandarins who have gone through a great deal of schooling. This is the thinking personality at work in a historical setting. That is the reason why the Chinese thinkers are given so much honor and that is why their society is built upon the thinker more than other societies. This thinking personality is usually intense and able to penetrate to the heart of the matter for the purpose of seeing how all things fit together so that there will come about a harmonious whole. The archetype of the China personality is an intense person who is very poised. Our picture of the Chinese personality is one in which the person presents a wise and thoughtful outlook upon reality, a person who is intense upon finding the natural harmony between all things and at the same time possesses the poise to bring about the harmony between man and his nature and between man and the reality.

When we entered the view of the third cause we entered the realm of Plato with emphasis upon the ideal and ways in which society could be bettered and in which more and greater virtues of mankind could be produced than the present world situation allowed. Plato also stressed the wise person who tries to find the way in which it would be possible to unite the purpose of this world with the purpose of the reality as a whole. The wise man according to Plato finds the ultimate laws and principles through study and he imparts these ultimate laws and principles into his society so that his society may follow in the correct footsteps as nature originally ordained. What Plato wished for in the Republic the Chinese actually accomplished in their view of the fourth cause. The ultimate purpose of the ruler in Plato can be found in the practices that the Chinese have developed for centuries. This does not come about by chance; a cause produces this effect and the fourth cause is the view from China, as the third and fourth cause is the view from Plato.

In all it should be remembered that each cause does not have a greater value than any other cause. It is necessary to have all four causes to produce the fulfillment of reality. But it should also be noted that a person viewing reality through a particular cause will naturally be inclined to think that his view is better than any other view and this is where conflict comes into reality. People who follow a view from the first cause live in a Tribal society and reality is viewed from the becoming phase. Those who view reality from the second phase think that they view things from the only correct vantage point and look upon the tribal society as primitive and incorrect. The view from the third cause presents a conflict with the first and second cause. That is why the people of America who represented the tribal or first cause had to be placed in reservations in which they could continue living their view, for there was no room for them in the society looking towards reality from the third cause. That was why the reformers had to leave the European society which still concentrated upon the second or the formal view of reality. So the same thing is presenting itself with those who view reality through the third cause, exemplified by the United States and those who view reality through the fourth cause, exemplified by the Asians and especially the Chinese. It seems that the four basic world personalities do not get along with each other.

Perhaps a good way of summing up the views of the four basic personalities is through the eyes of religion. The first cause or personality looks upon reality through the eyes of the Father and through traditions of the tribes. The second personality views reality though the eyes of the Son and the formal structure of reality. The third personality views reality through the eyes of the Holy Spirit and the motivational aspect of reality. The fourth personality views reality through the harmonous unity of this reality with the total reality seen and unseen, and this personality wishes to merge himself with the natural harmony of all things becoming a part of the total goodness of the reality.

THE FOUR CAUSES AND RELIGION

Religion is the formal structure by which people formulate their recognition of a reality and upon which this reality is dependent. Depending upon the cause in which the individual finds himself, this will be the way in which the person and the society will formulate their recognition of another reality. If the person lives in the first cause the recognition will favor the Father or the first cause. That is why when the Christian missionaries went to primitive tribes who were in the first cause or viewing reality from the first cause, the emphasis of the Christian religion was upon the Father. The missionaries were even called great white fathers. Those societies in the second cause place the emphasis of the religion upon the Son and His Mother; that is why the Church which stresses the formal or categorical structure places the emphasis upon the Son and the church itself is called Mother Church. The emphasis clearly is upon the second person and the second cause and the recognition of another reality is through the second cause so the second person is honored. The society that stressed the third cause such as the United States represents the third view of reality and religion and this view places the recognition of a higher reality upon the third person of the trinity, the Holy Spirit. The recognition is given through the third cause which places emphasis upon motion and the indwelling of the Spirit which motivates the person and the society to bring forth fruit.

The view from the fourth cause places the emphasis upon harmony and oneness, unity and wholeness that should exist between this reality and the reality which supports this reality. The Christian religion as of yet has not recognized the fourth method by which a society can give recognition to another reality but once it is understood that there can be four ways in which recognition can be given religiously and otherwise there will be no problem in finding ways to fit Christianity to the fourth viewpoint of reality. As a matter of fact Christianity fits into the fourth cause like a glove. There is in Christianity the ultimate goal of all things in this reality living together in peaceful harmony. There is the ideal projected by the Christian religion of the wolf lying down next to the sheep and all the other animals living together in a peaceful harmony. This idea is the same viewpoint of the fourth cause with all things living in harmony with each other and this reality conducting itself in harmony with all the other realities producing one harmonious whole for the total reality. Religion and the four causes . . . no problem.

MARTIN LUTHER AND THE THIRD CAUSE

Now that the dust is somewhat settling between the views of the Catholic and the views of the Reformers in the Christian Church we can see that one side placed the emphasis upon the second cause and the reformers were those who placed the emphasis upon the third cause.

Martin Luther emphasized the efficiency of the individual in matters of religious judgment. It was no longer necessary for the individual to rely upon the formal institutions to tell him how to live his life and how to interpret the bible. The individual was now considered an efficient person capable of doing and fulfilling his own destiny. The emphasis was no longer upon the "Mother" Church or the formal institution but upon the productive individual. The formal church placed emphasis upon the clerical people who operated the institution and upon the rules, the laws and the dogmas of religious beliefs. This institutional outlook was that of the second cause pure and simple. When the whole body of church members were referred to in print or in talk, the body was addressed as "the Priest and Religious and the Laity." The emphasis clearly is upon those who operate and execute the institutional body of the church and of the members who are not a part of the organization all are lumped under the term "laity." This attitude is perfectly correct with the view from the second cause for this view is that in which the development of the being of the Church is the main consideration and this was the consideration when the formal structure of the church was being developed in the Middle Ages. When this structure was developed and completed the world then turned from the formal development of the second cause to the fruitful development of the individual in the third cause and this is what Martin Luther is all about.

Martin Luther is in religious circles what Sir Thomas More is in political circles and what Descartes is in the intellectual realm. These three men and their followers put the emphasis upon the third cause, the cause which motivates the individual to produce something from himself and to attempt to fulfill himself as an individual. So we see in the story of these two viewpoints a slow separation of outlooks and interests. Europe which was and is closely associated with the views of the second cause and the emphasis upon the formal and the institutional geared itself to combat those who favored the views of the third cause and the result was a general migration of people who wanted to go some place to put their views into effect. The development of the United States with the emphasis upon the individual rights and his goal of fulfilling himself is the third cause. These causes are not something to take lightly for they are the very thing for which people live and die because they give an individual a definite view upon reality. Since Europe was committed to the view of the second cause a place had to be found to develop the view of the third cause and this opportunity was provided by the lands of the Americas. In effect then we have the four causes represented in this world at this time in four definite and distinct locations. The first cause is represented by the African nations who are now in a process of becoming. The second cause is represented by the European nations who emphasize the formal and the institutional and the categorical. The third cause is located in the United States and in the Americas generally with the emphasis upon the fulfillment of the individual person. The fourth cause is located in China and Asia which placed the emphasis upon the merging of the individual with the whole of the reality so that all would become as one, united and a whole.

NATURAL CONFLICT BETWEEN SECOND AND THIRD CAUSE

We have seen as a historical fact that there was much conflict between those who favored the second and those who favored the third cause. The fighting went on for generations and still after 400 years it continues to boil and churn among the advocates of one cause and another.

Marriage is a good example of this conflict. In a society which looks upon reality from the second cause, marriage is viewed as a formal contract, formalized by the Church making two persons into one identity and allowing a new method of operation. It is a legal and categorical union of two people. In the second view we are looking at the new oneness presented for development. We are looking at the new identity formed by the marriage and we are looking at the new operation which is to be developed. In other words we are looking through the eyes of the categories that will formalize the marriage. To consider breaking this development taking place through the categories would also be going against the whole society which is engrossed in the development of the second cause.

After 1500 A.D. the formation of the society was complete and a good percentage switched over to the third cause and those who did placed the emphasis upon the fulfillment of the individual person. The relationships of the individual person to other singular and individual persons were now given more consideration or rather were just beginning to receive more attention. The individual was also considering his own fulfillment and happiness and development. Turning now to the example of marriage, the society which places the emphasis upon the second cause will look upon marriage as something which must be developed through the categories and which is not to be dissolved at any cost because this would be going against the very outlook of the society. The society which views reality from the third cause will not be considering the formalization of the marriage but will view the marriage from the standpoint of the individuals involved. If it is found that one or both parties in the marriage is not treated as an individual and the partners do not have a good relationship or above all if the partners are not happy or fulfilled in the marriage then the marriage should be dissolved and the partners allowed to try again to seek their happiness and fulfillment as individuals. In the third cause the society will back the individuals in their attempt to seek fulfillment and happiness and that is why these societies who follow the third cause will have more divorce than those who view reality from the second cause. The stigma of breaking a formal contract or a formal categorical development is not considered to be of any great importance from the view of the third cause but it certainly is from the view of the second cause.

In the second cause, the male, who gives the name in marriage and who carries on the family name, is the one who is considered the important partner for it is he who makes the identification of the marriage. The view from the third cause considers each partner as equally important and so arises the view of equality in marriage. No longer is the emphasis placed upon the identity of the marriage but upon the happiness of each partner and consequently the marriage is looked upon as a contract between two equal persons with equal rights and obligations.

We should say something of the view from the first cause for this view expresses marriage in a different way also. The emphasis is solely and completely upon the father or the male with the female receiving no recognition whatsoever. In the first cause the emphasis is upon the father which brings forth a becoming or who allows a becoming to take place and this marriage expresses this view also as having the male or the father receiving the only consideration. In all things then each cause will express itself in a different manner with regard to marriage. Marriage in the fourth cause will be expressed in a different manner also. The emphasis will be upon the harmony of the individual with the ancestors of the past and the parents of the present and with the children who are the future.

CONFLICT SEEMS TO BE ALWAYS PRESENT BETWEEN THE CAUSES

We have seen that there is a conflict between the first cause and the second cause, between the second cause and the third cause, and there is a conflict between the third and the fourth cause.

In the first cause the conflict is between the traditionalists or those who wish to follow in the paths and the ways of the fathers of the tribes and clans. These traditionalists are like the founders of the Christian Church who continue to follow the rules of the fathers of the church and who favor the patriarchs' view of reality. Since the Greek church is the original founder of the Christian Church they view their religion from the view of the first cause and consequently it is from the view of the fathers or founders of the church.

The second view is in conflict with the first view for this view expresses reality through the being of the thing. This means the categorical development of the reality. This view expresses reality through institutions and organizations and social formal bodies. This is the view of the organizational man and the man who wishes to develop and place things in their proper categories. In the first cause we see the Fathers and founders of the church being opposed by the Pope and the order of organizational men who wish to instil all things and develop all things through categories. The first view wishes to instruct the society through the traditions and customs of the first cause. The second cause wishes to instruct mankind through the institutions of the church, the governments and the intellectual institutions which the second cause has developed.

The conflict between the second cause and the third cause is between those who wish all things to develop through the organization. The second cause says that you should follow the dictates of the organization and the authority who operates the organization and the institutions. The third cause says that a man is an individual and that he should follow his own conscience and that he alone should be the guide in fulfilling himself and seeking happiness. The organization wishes the individual to follow the orders and the rules of the institutions and the third cause says that in order for the individual to develop and produce something of himself he must follow the dictates of his own conscience and this will enable the person to be motivated to produce something from himself. The second cause cares little about the conscience of an individual for it is concerned with the development of the being through the categories, whereas the individual is deeply concerned with that which will motivate him to bring forth some fruits from his being. An artist best represents the third cause for he must have something in himself motivating him to bring forth some new creative thing from his own being. It is a deeply personal thing to bring forth a creation or product from the self. The formal church has never really felt at ease with artists because the artist takes his direction from something inside of him and the formal church is concerned with developing things through the institutions that it has developed, and naturally the two views feel a little uneasy with each other.

As there is a conflict between the first and second cause and the second and third cause so there will be a conflict between the third and the fourth cause. The fourth cause views reality through the eyes of one accustomed to seeing the oneness of all things, the goodness and the harmony of all things working and living together. In the third cause there will be a competitive atmosphere among the people for each individual will be trying to achieve his happiness or fullness and those who look upon the third cause from the view of the fourth cause will see nothing but grasping individuals all trying to achieve their own self interest. Those viewing the fourth cause from the third cause will see people who do not seem to have any interest in helping themselves and developing themselves. They will see a stagnant society with the younger people honoring what has gone before and following what is present with no inclination to change or develop or "progress" (the magic word of the third cause) themselves into a better society. The people of the third cause will sweep away all things in order to develop themselves and produce something from themselves while the members of the fourth cause will wish to live in close harmony with even the smallest creatures and will be reluctant to kill even the most lowly of insects.

To complete the cycle the fourth cause looks upon the first cause as something chaotic and barbaric and in which all things are in flux and a state of becoming. The view from the fourth cause has everything in a harmony and in which all things are good unto themselves and in conjunction with all other things. The view from the first cause is that of the Dark Ages of mankind which is in active rebellion against all things with no order or light and so begins the cycle again.

FOUR CAUSES AND THE INDIVIDUAL THING

We are studying the four causes in world history but it should never be lost sight of that the individual thing also goes through the cycle of four causes. History shows the working of the four causes on a larger canvas but the individual has the same cycle.

Every thing that lives a normal life span develops through the four causes. The becoming or the germination of the thing is the period of the first cause and this is the period of the entity. This is the Dark Ages of the individual for it is the period of the becoming in which the three major ingredients are developing into one human being. The water, the blood and the spirit are becoming a new one thing.

The second cause begins when the one thing is presented to the reality for development by the society in which it finds itself. This development takes place through the categories. There are nine categories and these are placed into three groups. The first group concerns the essence of the being. The essence develops the oneness of the thing. The existence develops the identity of the thing. The operation develops the completeness of the thing with the reality. The three categories in each group allow the three developments to take place. The categories are the paths which provide the principles of essence, existence and operation to develop the being. This is the second cause.

The third cause provides the values which will instil in the individual the motivational force to have him produce something from himself into the reality. The values enable the individual to consider himself as something unique and distinct from all other things and thus the responsibility is placed upon the individual to do something about the uniqueness and the singularity of his person. This places some value upon the relationships that the individual should have to be more productive so he is inclined to form mutual associations for more productiveness and efficiency. The person is happy or full when he is able to develop to the fulness of his potentiality and so he wishes to have as few restrictions as possible placed before him. It is freedom to develop which is a great value to those individuals of the third cause, which the individual must have if he is to develop his fullest possible productiveness and achieve his full individuality.

The fourth cause in the individual considers the purpose and the goals of the whole reality in this world and the totality of world seen and unseen. The fourth cause considers the oneness of the reality with all the parts playing and contributing toward this oneness. The fourth cause considers the unity of all things in this world and the unity of this world with other realms of reality. It considers the harmony of all things and how all things fit together into a unity with each thing contributing towards the harmony. The fourth cause considers the goodness of the reality and the goodness of the total reality in which this reality is part of that goodness. The fourth cause shows that the created is a part of the goodness of the creator and that all things that have been created as well as the creator are good in themselves and provide a wholeness for the total reality.

The first cause considers the child; the second cause considers the developing youth; the third cause considers the mature person; and the fourth cause considers the wise man. There is a cause providing a facet for every stage of development in the person, nothing is left to chance.

FOUR CAUSES IN THE BIBLE

In the first part of the historical rendition of the four causes we have seen that the four causes were at work in the development of the three ancient civilizations which eventually developed into the Western Civilization—Roman, Greek and Jewish understanding of the world.

In the New Testament we can see the four causes at work through the four Gospel writers. The first Gospel writer speaks of the coming of Christ as that which is the final result of the Old Testament. Matthew places the emphasis and view of the events leading up to the presentation of Christ as a historical figure. A long description is given as to who was related to the Christ in the ancient past, where Christ originated and the parents he came from.

Mark places emphasis upon the development of Christ as a historical figure, stressing that He is the Christ of the Old Testament for whom the Jews have waited so long. The emphasis is upon the identity of Christ.

Luke considers the Gospel for those who are interested in the third cause. He places the emphasis upon the fruits which should come forth from the followers of Christ and the fruits are those which are motivated through the Holy Spirit. The Holy Spirit is given full recognition and the emphasis is the working of the spirit in the person, and from the spirit the fruits of the person will come forth.

John considers the Gospel for those who consider the final cause of all things. The emphasis is upon the goal of unity of all Christians and the mutual exchange of love for all persons in this world. The oneness of the reality and the goodness of the reality is emphasized along with the necessity for being united with all men in a brotherhood of mutual love and consideration.

So again we see the working of the four causes in the historical setting of the religion of Christianity. The four causes are necessary to give a complete picture of the total reality and without the four causes something would be lacking in the presentation of the reality. First we are concerned with material ingredients; then we are concerned with the developed formal being; then we are concerned with the values and the fruition of this life; finally we are concerned with the purpose and the goals of this or any reality. These four causes give us a complete understanding of reality and fully present the reality to us.

SUMMING UP THE FOUR CAUSES IN HISTORY

In the overall picture of this world the becoming or the first cause presented itself in Africa where over a long period the human man was finally presented in this reality. It seems that the geographical place and the cause is more or less fixed. Africa to this day is still devoted to the becoming stage. We shall see that the same applies to other regions which have different causes.

When the full becoming of a man was achieved and there was presented to reality a one man, the next cause entered history and a new geographical region came under the spotlight. The Nile valley and the Middle East became the regions of development for the second cause. The social organizations of mankind were developed so that the development of the human being could take place. The social institutions were necessary because they allowed the categories to be presented and the categories allowed the development of the second cause to take place. This begins the period of the formal written history of mankind. It is through the three principles of essence which will develop the oneness of mankind; the existence with which the identity of mankind will take place and the operation in which the completeness of mankind was to be developed.

The second period ended with the coming together of the three major principles of development. The Roman government provided the essential development of mankind. This essential development provided for the full development of the oneness of mankind through one government and through one code of laws. The Greeks provided for the full existential development of mankind by developing all the methods by which mankind is capable of communication with his reality. The full identity of mankind is achieved through the various channels of the principle of existence. All the intellectual channels were developed and completed by the Greeks and this provided the fullest possible identity to be made with the reality in which man finds himself. The Hebrews developed the principle of operation in which the completeness of mankind was developed. This principle developed the regular habits which would complete mankind. The religious practices and all the other religious observances were the regulatory actions which were the highest development in the operation of mankind. The emphasis is upon the chosen people and the place of these people in the scheme of things. A set of moral laws was developed to fit the circumstances of the life and thus the operation of mankind was developed and the completeness of humanity was occomplished by the Hebrew religion and the Hebrew emphasis upon the operational principle of the second cause.

Surprisingly enough if anyone wants to know what an essence is all about, all he has to do is study the Roman government. This is the historical development of the essence of mankind. The Roman government was concerned with bringing about the full development of the material oneness of mankind. Through the development of the one law and one form of government which would be capable of ordering the material goods and services of the whole of mankind the principle of essence was fully developed. Presently one form of laws generally embrace the entire world except China and Turkey. Roman Law allows all nations in this world to have relationships with each other and allows for the distribution of goods and services. When China and Turkey enter full relationships with the rest of the world they also will adopt Roman Law. This then is what the principle of essence is all about: the development of the material oneness of mankind historically and individually.

If anyone wants to know what existence is, Greeks have presented the full development of this principle. All the ways and manners possible for mankind to communicate and identify with this reality were fully developed and completed by the Greeks. Through their language, literature, arts, poetry, theater, philosophy, theology and all the other forms of expression the Greeks presented the full development of this principle. There is not one manner of expression which the Greeks had not developed. This achievement allowed mankind to fully identify himself with himself and with the reality in which he was associated with. The communication with the self and with the reality allows the principle of existence to develop. To communicate, associate and participate in the reality in which one finds himself . . . this is existence. This is the Greek experience.

If anyone wishes to see what operation is all about on stage he will have to look at the Hebrew history. The Hebrews concentrated upon the principle of operation in which the emphasis was upon the regular religious observances which had to be performed in a prescribed manner. The repeated and the regular observance of these religious practices were considered of ultimate importance. Instilled in the history of these people was the idea of place or position. These people had a chosen place or position in this and the unseen reality. Place and position is repeatedly emphasized. The history of these people placed great emphasis upon the place of the individual. The place or the position allows the individual to operate more fully than a meaner place in this life. These people developed a set of moral rules and laws which allowed them to face any and all circumstances of life and this enabled them to carry on the full development of the operation of mankind. The development of the operation allowed the completeness of mankind to be achieved. This principle of operation enabled mankind to have a fully developed being. The principle of operation informs mankind that it is necessary to perform repeated and regular religious observances, that all things have a place and a position in this reality and nothing is unnecessary, and that to face the circumstances of life one must have a set of moral rules and regulations. This is the Jewish experience.

These three historical principles slowly came together

at the birth of Christ and thus the full development of the being of mankind was achieved. The formal development was accomplished. Each principle concerned itself with three categories. The Roman principle of essence concerned itself with the categories of quantity, quality and the relationships. In modern day usage this is the concern of the goods and the services that the governments provide for their people. The relationships is the just distribution of these goods and services.

The Greek principle concerns itself with the categories of receptivity, activity and time. To communicate fully with the reality in which one finds oneself one must be receptive to the reality and one must act upon the reality by giving reality some form or design. The Greeks gave a design to the reality that they communicated with and this design is the fullest development that mankind has yet achieved and will achieve. Man impressed his identity upon this reality to the fullest development and the identity of this reality and man was completed by the Greeks. By being receptive to this reality and acting upon this reality in time allowed the full development of identity between man and his reality.

The categories that the Jewish personality developed were the habits, places and circumstances of the principle of operation. Instilling in the people the repeated observances of certain practices; emphasis upon the chosen people and their place in this reality and the reality beyond this world; the moral set of laws and customs which allowed them to face the circumstances of this world: these categories allowed the full development of the operation of a human being.

The birth of Christ thus completed the second cause of mankind in which the full development of the being of mankind was completed. One government for the whole of mankind was established. Complete identity with the reality was established through the Greek achievement; and the completeness and the totality of the being was achieved by the Jews by providing the proper habits, a place in this reality and a set of laws which would govern the actions

123

of the person in all circumstances of this life. This completed the development of the being of man.

The third period of mankind begins with the third cause and this cause will place the emphasis upon motion and the fruition of mankind. The bringing forth of fruits will be the concern and the effect of this cause. This cause is concerned with motivating the individual person to produce something from himself and to bear fruit. Thus the beginning of the writing of biography and the lives of great saints come upon the historic scene. The works of the individual person and his life slowly gather momentum. The life of Saint Augustine is written by the great saint to show to the world what it was that motivated him to do the things that distinguished him. The coming of the primitive people into the Roman-Greek-Jewish civilization started to bring forth new fruits to humanity and slowly these people started to build their own civilization devoted to the fruition of mankind. Western Civilization is thus concerned with the third cause. The emphasis upon the individual and his relationship with this reality and the reality beyond this world and the fullness of the individual person is the main driving force of the Western Civilization.

Naturally any society goes through the four causes but the whole of mankind also goes through the four causes. The first cause beginning in Africa and the second cause beginning in the Middle East, and now the third cause which is represented by the Western Society and the fourth cause is represented by the Chinese and the Asians. In any given society the four causes also will be operating as will they be in any given thing or individual.

The four causes can thus be seen in the overall picture of mankind universally speaking. They can be seen in the general picture of mankind such as any society or culture. The four causes can be seen in the specific picture of mankind such as a definite society such as the Romans, Greeks or Jews or Americans. Finally the four causes can be seen in the life of the individual person through the four periods in which the person develops in this life. It will be noted that in the life of a very holy person after the completion of the fourth cause in which the person has achieved a high degree of harmony with the total reality he or she does not terminate his individuality by dying but is often said to ascend into another reality. Thus the completion of the final or fourth cause has nothing to do with the termination of one's individuality but rather with the complete harmonization of the self with the rest of reality, especially the unseen reality.

Looking at the history of our Western Civilization we can see the four causes operating. The first cause presented itself in the form of the coming primitive people such as the Franks, Goths, Alemanni, Visigoths, Vandals, Slavs, Alans, Ostrogoths, Saxons, Lombards, Sueves, Armenians, Angles, Huns and probably many more smaller tribes who offered the new material for a becoming society. After 500 years of development which was the Dark Ages of this society there was presented around 1000 A.D. a new society to be developed by the second cause which was the Middle Ages. This period of development also lasted for 500 years and the new society was fully formed and developed in this period. So entered the third period in which the emphasis was upon the fruition of the individual, and what motivated the individual person to accomplish and to bring forth fruits and to produce products from his being. This period of our society is slowly coming to an end for it has lasted for 500 years and enough emphasis has been given the individual to accomplish his productiveness. So in Western society the fourth period is beginning to present itself in which the oneness of the society and of all mankind will be emphasized. The unity of all men and the harmony of all men will be emphasized and also the goodness of all things rather than the sinfulness and the evilness. The positive aspects of reality will be given greater recognition rather than the negative aspects. As the fourth period is entered a closer relationship with China will be accomplished because of the overall picture of mankind it is the Chinese who have emphasized the fourth cause of reality.

125

The West will be in a better position to understand the ideas and the motives of China once it enters the fourth in its own society.

THE CAUSES AND THE REST OF THE WORLD

The question may be raised that in our mention of causes and certain geological locations a great percentage of the world population has been overlooked. We have used examples that are known and somewhat familiar to those of the West. We have not mentioned lands such as India or South America because they have not been in the mainstream of Western history. India is in its finalized cause and the lands of South America are more or less in the becoming cause even though they have a veneer of Western culture. Whenever there is a predominance of tribal customs the society is still in the becoming cause. Institutions and forms of government, schools and religion must come from the society and not be imposed from the outside as is the case of South America.

Europe can be divided into certain areas which show to this day the various causes working. The lands of Scotland, Ireland and Wales still emphasize the clannish and the tribal customs and they appear at times to still possess elements of the becoming cause. They have not completely left the first cause but still retain some of the flavor of the clannish or tribal period.

In the Western civilization certain segments continue to represent a particular cause even though the civilization as a whole has passed on to another cause. For instance Ireland and Scotland can be said to still emphasize the first cause in the society. These lands still place emphasis upon the families, the clans and the tribal viewpoint of reality. The viewpoint of the clans and the tribes and the strong families is the view from the first cause. This view looks upon the reality from the becoming standpoint and in the larger picture of mankind this can be seen through the tribal view of the Jewish people who continue to this day

to look upon reality from a becoming standpoint. The Jews
are looking for the coming of the Messiah. The tribal viewpoint looks upon reality through the becoming phases with
the ultimate goal of achieving actual oneness. Looking for
the coming of the Messiah is a looking for the effect of oneness, identity and completeness of the society. The Jewish
society has always found it difficult to have their own one
actual society, their own identity and their own completeness because there was always some other society trying
either to rule them or to break them up and so to this very
day their outlook upon reality is still from the view of the
first cause of becoming with the hope of achieving an actual
being of a society. So also in the Western society there are
areas in which the view still is from the first cause. We
can also see that today in our world the Jews have an opportunity to achieve this oneness of their society; this
identity and this completeness of their society through the
new state of Israel. Because of this historic happening in
which the Jews were prevented from realizing an actual
oneness, unity and operation there has been to this day
the view of reality from the becoming phases of reality.
Always looking at reality through the view of effecting a
society with all the tribes gathered together into one essential government; with all these tribes having a unity and
one identity; and with operation as a society in which there
is a completeness of the society, this has been the goal of
the Jewish people since their historic coming upon the
scene of history and this ultimate achievement has always
slipped from their hands.

The second view of society can be viewed from the
Spanish outlook. Spain and perhaps other portions of Europe still view much of reality from the second cause. This
view expresses the formative or the institutional outlook
and in Spain the government, the church and the schools
are the main ways of expressing oneself. The monarchy still
rules Spain if not in fact at least in sentiment. A monarchy
is the type of government which is associated with the
formative or the second cause. The Catholic Church which

represents the formative phases of the Christian Religion is well expressed in the society and the intellectual institutions favor the classical teaching rather than the technical and scientific training as a society which is in the third or productive phases of reality. Spain is sealed off from Europe by mountains and this has stopped the development of the third cause from entering into Spanish history to a great extent. To this day Spain still tries to prevent the reform of the productive phase of Christianity from entering the lands. The hue and cry against modern ideas or modernism is the cry from the second cause against the third cause taking over the society. The productiveness and the fruition of the individual in the Spanish view is not considered as important as it is in the United States, which is the best picture of the third view. Europe with its schools and its great churches and its monarchy-governments represents to a great extent the view of the second cause and it is pretty hard to get a clear picture of what the third cause represents from the European scene. That is why we have to go to the United States for a clear picture of the third cause in operation in a society.

THE THIRD CAUSE AND THE UNITED STATES

Governments, intellectual schools and religions walk softly in the third cause. In the third cause the emphasis is upon the development and the fruition of the individual and this view brooks little or no interference with the three formal structures of society: the governments, schools and religion.

The United States is the best example of the third cause in a society. The "American Way" of life is for the individual to develop himself to the fullest and to achieve as much happiness as possible. This emphasis is even in the constitution of the country. Government interference has always been a cry from those who follow the view from the third cause. The "individualists" or reformers from the Protestant Reformation left the European scene because

128

there the historical outlook was and is upon the formal governments, upon the formal or classical schools and upon the formal religious. It was in the United States especially that the individualists started their society which allowed for the individual to develop to the greatest extent possible. The government best suited to conduct the affairs of the third cause is that of the democratic type in which all members of the society are allowed to participate in some manner or form. Formal schools are not favored in the third cause and an outsider may get the feeling that the society is anti-intellectual. This is not the true situation at all for the society wants schools but it wants schools which will allow the individual to produce something. For this reason the United States has the best technical schools in the world and the best scientific institutions that the world has known. It is through science and the technical schools which teach the individual to do something that the society favors more than the formal schools which place the emphasis upon the development of the individual.

Science as we understand it today is that body of knowledge which allows men to bring forth something and to produce something from the individual. This type of knowledge is based upon the third view or the third cause of reality.

Formal or classical knowledge is designed with the second view in mind. The purpose of the formal or classical knowledge or training is to develop the being through the categories and the ultimate result is to have the being more of a developed one thing; to allow the being to have more identity with the reality in which the being finds itself; and to offer a completeness and totality to the being by and through the intellectual understanding of reality.

The formal or classical schooling was developed during the historical period in which the formal development of mankind was taking place. This was the period in which the essence was being developed which provided for one material government which would be capable of governing the whole of mankind. The intellectual classification of mankind was developed to the fullest by the Greek culture and finally the religious development was completed by the Jewish religion.

We of the Western world are not in the formal development of mankind as were the Romans, Greeks and Jews. We are in the fruitional phase of mankind and so the schools which we have developed are those which place emphasis upon the fruitional or the productiveness of mankind. Fruitional knowledge or as it is called "science" is the understanding appropriate to the third cause and it is especially appropriate to the United States which offers a clear cut picture of the working of the third cause in a society.

In schools which are devoted to the training of the classical or second phase of reality to the students, the students are given grades which show how much they have produced or how they have accomplished in their studies. Classical or formal schooling was and is to develop the being of the human person. It was not designed to produce grades or to bear fruit. The technical science or understanding was and is designed just for this purpose and its ultimate purpose is to produce some fruits. Since we are living the third or fruitional period of mankind especially in the United States there has been much confusion over the role of the formal or classical training and that of the fruitional training or the sciences. To think in terms of development of the being when the rest of the society thinks in terms of producing something naturally will bring about some confusing results. The classical or the developmental schools will place grades as the object of their education and the result will be the emphasis upon grades as the fruits of classical studies. Since the sciences do produce something in goods and services to mankind, the classical schools can say that they produce grades.

This confusion can all be avoided through the understanding of the causes. The classical schools are designed to develop the being to the fullest possible extent. The scientists and the technical people are interested in bringing forth the greatest amount of fruits or production. The classical is interested in the second cause and the scientific is interested in the third cause of reality.

The same confusion exists somewhat between those who follow the second cause in religion and those who favor the formal religion which places the emphasis upon the institutional structure of the church such as the Catholic Church exemplifies or those who favor the third cause which places the emphasis upon the perfectibility or the fruitional aspect of the individual and the working of Divine Grace to allow the individual to be motivated to produce something of merit from his being. The "fruitionalists" or the Protestants are naturally the predominant religion in the United States because this society is slanted towards the third view of reality while Europe by and large is still slanted towards the second view.

The fruitional Christians place the emphasis upon what the individual person can and should be doing to foster his religious beliefs and convictions. The church structure is composed of many small individual church groups. These small church groups best express the views of the individual members of the church. A formal church such as the Catholic Church expresses the views of the philosophers and theologians and the dogmas of belief of the institution. The formal church is generally not suitable to motivate the individual person to produce something from himself unless he become a part of the formal structure such as a priest, monk, brother or nun. The fruitional church on the other hand stresses the individual's contribution to the religion and favors the individual devoting time to the goals of his religion. Protestant Churches favor the individual devoting several years to overseas or missionary work while the formal or Catholic Church would have only its religious members perform such work with the non-religious contributing their "prayers" and money. The formal church desires of its individual members participation one step removed from the actual religious work of the church and the fruitional church desires of its members individual participation. It should always be kept in mind that each church allows for a positive participation of its individual members but each does so in a different way because of the different view upon reality.

MOVING ALONG

We have seen that first cause was and still is emphasized in the area of Africa and the Australian primitives of the stone age. This is the Southern view of reality and it is the view expressing the becoming of mankind, for this area is where mankind started.

The Northern view is that the cradle of civilization or development was the Mediterranean Basin. In the Northern view the second phase of mankind was achieved. The essential of mankind was developed in which the material oneness of mankind was accomplished when the Roman government was developed which allowed all the peoples of the world to be under one form of law and government. The complete identity of mankind was expressed in Greek intellectual development. The Jewish people contributed to the development of the religious completeness of mankind. So ended the second phases in the development of mankind.

Leaving the Northern second phases and entering the Western zone of mankind we enter upon the fruitional aspects of mankind and the third cause. Germany, France, Sweden, Denmark, England and the United States are the representatives of the third cause at work in our present historical view.

When we have left the Western zone we will naturally arrive in the Eastern zone which not surprisingly will be viewing reality from the fourth view or cause. This fourth historic view will be concerned with the oneness of all nature in which the being of man participates as a part of the totality of creation. The unity of the being with the total reality and the goodness of the total reality will be the achievements attempted by this view upon reality.

Since the United States is the best clear cut picture of the third cause and the mainland of China is the best clear cut picture of the fourth cause it is natural that the two views will come into conflict on the world stage as the first

132

view came in conflict with the second view and as the second view came into conflict with the third cause and view and so the view of the third cause is now coming into conflict with the fourth view. As with all world views the material comes first, the intellectual comes second and the religious comes third. So the material conflict with governments start the clash of views and after the governmental or material there is the philosophical and the intellectual meeting of minds and then the religious confrontation of the two views until there comes about a mutual understanding between members of the two parties to respect the views of the other so that some kind of harmony will come about. This is what eventually will happen between the United States and the Chinese world view as it has happened between the view of the second and third cause and between the first and the second world view.

It can also be seen that each new view expresses something that the other view has left out in the overall presentation of mankind in reality. The view from the first cause places the emphasis upon the becoming or the father aspect or the tribal and family aspect of reality with no emphasis upon the development of the being. The second view places the emphasis upon the development of the institutions of government, intellectual schooling and religion with no emphasis upon the development of the individual. The third attitude places the emphasis upon the development and the fruition of the individual with no emphasis upon the contribution that the individual plays in the total reality. The fourth cause places the emphasis upon the totality of reality and shows the part that each individual plays in the oneness, unity and the whole of the totality of beings in this and the unseen reality. So the four causes express the complete view of reality.

CHINESE PERSONALITY

It was mentioned that each view of reality presents a basic personality which best expresses that view and which best achieves the effect of that view.

133

The first cause presents a personality based upon courage. It requires courage to bring about a becoming and this is the archetype personality expressed by the first cause. In all becoming societies it is the warrior or the fighter which best expresses the hoped for achievement of the society. It is the man of warrior disposition who brings about some new becoming from a chaos. The people of Africa and all areas which express the becoming view have as their archetype or model that of the courageous fighter or sword bearer.

The second personality or archetype is the dynamic personality which looks upon reality with the view of constructing or development. This is the personality expressed by the people of the Mediterranean basin. This group of people developed the categories of human nature in which the formation of mankind was allowed to be achieved. The construction of governments, of intellectual understanding and the operation of religions were effected by these people.

The third personality is represented by the archetype being who is flexible. This personality is represented by the Western civilization in which the being is able to produce and to bring forth fruits of all kinds and descriptions. This personality is ingenious and is able to adapt to all sorts of conditions and to produce products which are applied to any and all endeavors in the society. From computers to the radio and the mechanical methods of farming this personality has brought forth methods and inventions which are able to increase the fruits of the earth and multiply production of things to an extent never before achieved. We are living in the days of this personality and this is the personality of Western Man and especially the personality of the United States. As the African developed the becoming of man or the first cause, and the Romans, Greeks and Jews developed the being or the second cause of mankind so Western Man has concentrated on the development of the third cause with which the fruition of mankind is allowed to take place and in which the individual is allowed to achieve the fullness of his individuality.

We now come to the personality that is the archetype of the Eastern people and especially China. The Chinese people have as their archetype that of the thinking personality. Their whole history has been one in which the thinker has led the nation and the people throughout her long historical journey. This personality is serious and intense. An example of the personality can be seen in their method of fighting such as Judo and Karate. These methods depend upon concentration and discipline and especially an intense personality to allow the method to work. The intensity of the archetype personality is offset by poise. A personality that is intense can be stiff but with poise also being a common trait the result is a very pleasing personality.

An example of this personality can be seen in the Chinese artist. The Chinese artist singles out one or two things from nature and intensifies this thing or things by drawing the thing not connected with any surrounding reality, thus the thing drawn is intensified. The natural disposition of the Chinese personality is to think about the thing first and then to concentrate all attention upon the object. The result is that the personality is able to bring forth a presentation of reality that is intensified in its singularity but at the same time is connected with the rest of the reality as a member.

It has been observed that the Chinese rely upon the ability of the person in the conduct of affairs of the state and not upon those born to the position. They have consistently sought the wise man to direct and to conduct their affairs. This truly was and probably still is the land in which the philosopher is the king as Plato wished his ideal republic to conduct their affairs. This is one of the reasons they have had such a long and continuous history. The Chinese personality has always run parallel with the harmony of nature in union with the pulse of reality.

From this presentation of reality we can see and also say that there are four views upon which one may understand reality. The first view is that of the first cause of becoming concerning the tribal view of reality. The second view is that of the institutional government, school and church and this is the formal view. The third is that of the individual and his relationship with the reality in which he finds himself. The fourth view is that of the totality of the reality and the harmony and the goodness of the reality. So what have we but four views of the truth. The whole truth is the totality of the four causes.

We are all pointed in one direction because of being born into a society which is pointed in that direction. We can be born into a society looking to the south and the first cause. We may have been born into a society looking at the north or the second or formal cause. We could have been born in the western society and be pointed to the third cause of reality or the fruitional or productive side of reality. We could have been born into the fourth side and be pointed towards the east looking at the reality though the eyes of harmony and the realization and finalization of the fourth cause.

GOVERNMENTS: SCHOOLS: CHRISTIANITY

The three areas which express the oneness, unity and wholeness of the human condition work in conjunction with each other through the cause prevailing in the society at the time. In the first cause the government will center around the tribal system or clan and the rule will be by the father figure or the petty chieftain. The schools will consist of lore and experience handed down from the father to the son and mother to daughter. The religion will be that of the fathers of the church or that which follows the ritual and traditions of the founders. This is the religion similar to the Eastern Rite Christian Church. The Eastern or to be more exact the Middle Eastern, follows the first cause to this day in its adherence to the traditions and manners of the founding fathers of the Christian Church.

The three ingredients of the society thus look upon reality from the first cause and each expresses the first cause through their manner of doing things. Their whole expression is through the fathers of the clan or tribe, through the experience of the ancient and the elders and the father and mother, and through the founding fathers of the church or religion of the society.

The second cause presents a different view and so do the governments, schools and religion. The governments are made up of nobles and limited monarchy. The emphasis is upon the development of social structure and the institutions of government. The schools began to become formalized and institutionalized and there begins the categorization of all learning and we begin to see the writing of books which try to sum up all the knowledge of the period and put it into a systematic form. The church develops the institutions and the structure of organization and this is expressed by the Roman Catholic Church with the emphasis upon the organizational structure with the Pope as the head of the structure.

All these three are the principles of development of the society and they participate in the formal development of the society which is the end effect of the second cause.

In the third cause the society begins to emphasize the individual and the result is that the governments begin to elevate the individual to great heights. The days of the autocrat or the divine rule of the king begin. The Christian Church begins to emphasize the individuality of the person or member and there results the formation of a new branch of the Christian Church which places the emphasis upon the third cause and this is the protestant or the fruitional branch of the Christian Church. The schools also begin to change over to the third cause and the emphasis is upon learning that can produce something from the reality in which the individual finds himself. The scientific learning begins to become the dominant form of instruction because it is that type of learning which is able to bring forth new products and new things into the reality. This is the knowledge needed for the fruitional period or the third cause.

In the fourth cause the problems are again a little different and so will be the view from the governments, the schools and the religion. The government will be that which resembles the government of Rome during the days of the Caesars. This is a cosmopolitan form of government which considers the whole reality and the harmony of the government with the total reality. This form of government is that which the Chinese have emphasized from their very beginning. It is a government which places the emphasis upon the harmony and the unity and the goodness of the totality of society in contradistinction to the third cause which places the emphasis upon the individuality or the rights of the individual.

The schools will try to install and teach the understanding of the interrelationship between all things and the part that all things play in the totality of the world order. The schools will place the emphasis upon the harmony that should be present between all things in this reality and the unseen reality.

The Christian Church in the fourth cause will express the goodness of the reality. In the Middle Eastern Church the emphasis was upon the traditions of the founders and following the rites of the becoming church. The Catholic Church placed the emphasis upon the classification of the sins and the evils that prevail in the society along with the classification of the virtues that the Christian should achieve. In the fruitional church the emphasis was upon the fruits or the production of the individual. In the fourth Christian Church the emphasis is upon the goodness of the totality of things in this society and in the reality that is not experienced.

We can see that the government, the schools and the church again work in conjunction with each other, each looking upon reality from the same view point yet expressing a distinct facet of the prevailing view.

Each cause demands a different form of government, a different form of schooling and the different structure in the church. In all causes it is still necessary to have governments, schools and churches. The governments express the oneness of the reality in all the causes. The schools express the identity of the society in all the causes and the churches express the completeness and the wholeness of the society in all the causes. The thing to remember is that each cause demands a different expression of these three goals of oneness, unity and wholeness.

CHINESE AND THE FOURTH CAUSE

The Chinese are a good example of the working of the fourth cause. They have not developed a system of logic which is associated with the second cause nor have they placed much importance on epistemology which is connected with the third cause dealing with the individual and his relationship to his reality. The Chinese always have been concerned with what man IS rather than what he can produce or own. The Chinese school of thought has been primarily devoted to the quest for the final solution of human problems. The Chinese place the conduct of government upon the personal equation of group conscience. In the Western countries which place the emphasis upon the individual and his paying heed to laws and conventions, the Chinese in their turn place the emphasis upon the oneness of all mankind and the harmony that should exist between all peoples. Chinese civilization places the emphasis upon cosmopolitanism as the ultimate aim of the government, and this foundation is built upon complete fairness between individuals. The mainstream of Chinese thought has been the emphasis upon the central harmony, the cordial relationships between Nature and man, the preservation of one's life and the full realization of one's nature, of mental tranquility, and the interaction of the active and the passive in man and his nature and finally the fundamental goodness of human nature. These are the ultimate goals of the fourth cause and this is what the Chinese have been striving to accomplish.

FOUR POINTS OF THE COMPASS

It is hoped that one may understand that the divine plan for the understanding of reality is that which is viewed through the four points of the compass, which represent the four causes. There is a definite place in which to view reality. If one lives in the south of this world, the view will be from the first cause or the becoming of things. If the view is from the Middle East or really the north because it is north of the equator, the view is that of the second cause which is concerned with the development of the being of the reality. If the view is that from the west then the emphasis will be upon the individuality and the fruition of the individual. When the view is that of the east then the emphasis will be upon the realization of the reality with the total reality, and the harmony between all things. There is a definite point in this world and if a person is living within a particular point then he will be viewing reality from that point. We are born in a certain place and it is from that place which we view reality and each place emphasizes a definite cause.

A good example of the four causes as they operate in a society can be seen by using the four stroke engine as a background for this process. The four strokes of the engine are called the *intake, compression, power* and *exhaust.* In the beginning of the society all the new blood is being taken into the society such as the Romans taking in the barbarian tribes and clans during the latter days of the Empire. The great influx of new blood shatters the fragile and exhausted government and the new blood starts to become a new society during their period of Dark Ages. When all the new blood is fully ingested into the becoming society then the first stroke or the *intake* ends and the second stroke beings. The *compression* stroke forms and develops the new blood into a stable society which begins to be identified as something distinct from all other societies and begins to operate independently from any and all other societies. This is the period of the Middle Ages which brings about the creation and development of the formal structure of the society. Next comes the *power* stroke or the third cause. This is the stroke which produces the scientific exploration of the world and the inventions and the discoveries. The beginning of the industrial system begins to formulate and the fruits of the society begin to come forth. This is the period of our dynamic civilization and this is the period which we have been living since 1500 A.D. In the fourth period we enter the *exhaust* stroke or the finalization stroke. The *exhaust* stroke concerns itself with waste products and the realization of the society. Waste of human resources is beginning to be a concern of the society because there is no longer the emphasis upon the power and products and waste and pollution is beginning to be considered by the society in larger measure. In the fourth cause the individual is now considered along with the environment in which he finds himself and he is considered a part of the team or a part of the unity of the whole society. The right of the individual is no longer given consideration as during the power stroke. It is the harmonization of the whole social order that is the order of the day, and the goal of the society.

THE CONCEPTION OF THE SUPREME BEING ACCORDING TO THE FOUR CAUSES

Since each view of reality offers a distinct picture of the total reality it is to be expected that the concept of a supreme being will naturally be different with each view. In the first view the supreme being will resemble that of the all powerful father figure. The outlook will be upon the father from which all things come. The patriarch of the tribe will be the outstanding figure of this point of view. This is the first view of the trinity and it is looking

141

upon the first person of the trinity for it is from the first person that the beginning of all things are allowed to come about.

The view of the supreme being in the second cause will naturally place the emphasis upon the second person of the supreme trinity and this will be the Son. The formal church places the most emphasis upon the Son or Christ who formulated the whole of mankind. It is the son who is concerned with the development of this reality and the whole of reality. That is why Aristotle was introduced in the Middle Ages because he placed the emphasis upon the formation of things and this is the realm in which the second person contributes to the society and to the reality.

The view of the supreme being for those of the third cause will naturally be that of the third person the Holy Spirit. The spirit will be stressed in theology and we can see this in the fruitional church in which the emphasis is upon the indwelling or the overcoming by the spirit. This third cause places much emphasis upon the indwelling of the spirit which will bring about the fruits of the individual. It is the power of the spirit in which the individual hopes to bring forth some fruits from his individuality. There is much emphasis upon overpowering by the spirit and hearing the voice of the spirit so that the individual will produce some good in his life.

The view from the fourth cause will naturally be different from the other three views. There will be no emphasis upon a particular person of the trinity. The view will be from the concept of mankind living in harmony with the whole of reality, the seen and the not seen, the experienced and the not experienced, trying to harmonize the society and the individual so that the whole reality will perform as one; so that the totality will have one identity in which all things have some degree of communication with each other from the smallest to the grandest. This outlook embraces the whole reality in creation and out of creation. There is no distinction between the

142

created and the creator but all is considered as belonging to one whole which is good.

Each view of reality is correct considering the cause and the window through which the society is looking. Each view expresses something that the other views are not capable of expressing. Each view expresses a total truth and a total view. The understanding of the four causes allows one to have a conception of the total understanding of reality. It will be seen that in each cause something is to be accomplished. The first cause does the planting. The second cause does the watering and developing. The third cause does the work or the harvesting; and the fourth cause does the harmonizing of this reality with the total reality. Each cause, each period of time, each point of the compass accomplishes a definite goal and achieves a definite result.

Man is not placed on this earth or in this reality to sit and dream but to accomplish definite goals and definite programs. Man has a free choice and he may or may not participate in the program, and this is where the rub comes in, for some do and some don't participate but the programs and the goals are to be accomplished all the same and they are being accomplished, whether most people know about them or not makes little or no difference.

DEFINITIONS

Cause: An all inclusive and all embracing presentation of reality. A cause presents something distinct towards which the society strives to accomplish.

Four causes necessary for reality: There are four distinct and separate causes needed to produce the whole of reality. Each cause supplies something exclusive and distinct from the other three causes.

Cause does not produce another cause: There must be four causes present at all times in order to have a full reality. The first cause does not produce the second cause as its effect. The first cause makes it mandatory that there be a second cause and so forth.

Entity: Entity concerns the first cause and it is the universal concept of the first cause. It represents something in the process of becoming universally speaking. It is not actually determined but it is in the process of leading up to the presentation of actuality.

Possible or Potential: This is the general concept of the first cause and concerns the opportunity for some reality to become. If something is not possible there could be no reality.

Substrate: The substrate is the specific foundation that supports the becoming of a specific thing. The substrate specifies the becoming that is taking place.

Matter: The first major requirement needed for any individual becoming.

Form: The second major requirement needed for any individual becoming.

Motion: The third major requirement needed for any individual becoming.

Matter: Form: Motion: The three major material ingredients which are responsible for the individual becoming. The first cause is concerned with the material ingredients needed so that a becoming can take place.

Becoming: Something in the process of becoming one distinct thing. Becoming is a process in which the material ingredients are developing together in order to produce a new one thing to the reality.

Being: The thing which is presented to the reality after the first cause is completed. The being is the effect of the first cause and the problem of the second cause is to form and develop this being.

Actual: Some thing that is actually presented in a reality to be determined and developed. This is the general effect of the second cause as the being is the universal effect of the second cause.

Substance: This is the specific effect of the second cause. The substance is that which is presented to our realm of experience. The substance is that which is specifically to be determined and developed by the third cause.

Essence: Is the principle through which the development of the oneness of the being is to take place. Essence is that principle which is concerned with the formation of the materiality of the thing into one definite thing.

Existence: The principle of existence is concerned with the development of the identity of the thing. It is concerned with developing communication between the thing and the reality so that an identity can be developed and formed.

Operation: The principle of operation is concerned with development of the complete thing as an independent actual thing. This principle is concerned with developing the habits and finding the place and developing the moral rules which would allow the being to act independently of any other supporting reality. The principle completes the development of the being.

Essence: existence: operation: There are three principles through which the being can develop and these principles harbor the categories through which the being is developed. Each principle contains three categories.

Fruition: The third cause in its universal sense concerns the fruition or production of the reality. The fruition of reality concerns the efficiency of the producing thing.

Idealization: This is the general value which is presented by the third cause. The universal value is the bringing forth of some fruit. This is the universal value presented by the third cause. The general value is the ideal which is presented to the individual to allow him to bring forth some fruit from his individuality.

Illumination: This is the specific value which is presented by the society as the specified thing to produce by the individual. Illumination is the values or the package of values which the society or the reality presents to the individual to motivate the individual to produce something from himself.

Singularity: This is the individual value which motivates the individual by stressing the uniqueness of the person and instills upon the individual the responsibility of bringing forth fruits from his being.

Relationships: This is the individual value which motivates the person to seek relationships with other beings so that a greater and more efficient productivity can come forth from the individual. This value stresses the necessity of working with others to bring about a greater productivity than would be possible through the individual alone.

Fulness: This individual value motivates the individual to bring forth something from himself which gives the individual an understanding of completeness. The giving of oneself allows the individual to experience a fulness of his person and a measure of happiness. This

147

individual value answers the question, What's in it for me?

Singularity: Relationship: Fulness: These three major values allow the individual to bring forth fruits from his individuality. The value of individuality places responsibility upon the individual. The value of relationships allows a greater production to come forth; and the value of fulness allows the individual satisfaction in bringing forth something from his person.

Purpose: The universal goal of the fourth cause is to achieve the ultimate purpose in this or any reality. The purpose is the universal concept of the fourth cause and it concerns the finalization of the thing.

Realization: The general goal of the fourth cause is the realization of the thing with itself and with the rest of reality.

Substantialization: This is the specific goal of the fourth cause. This concerns the things which we experience in our practical reality. The specific thing which is to be finalized is that thing which had a becoming, a being and an individuation and now a realization. This is our specific goal.

One: This is the individual goal of the fourth cause. This is the goal of the individual to become one with the reality in which he finds himself and to become one with the total reality.

Unity: This is the goal of the thing to become united with the total reality in which the thing becomes a part and participator in the totality of things. All the parts become united together and form one identity and this identity is the total reality.

Whole: This is the third individual ultimate goal of the fourth cause. This goal seeks to achieve a total reality which is a whole and which is a good. The wholeness of the reality is the achieving of the complete goodness of the thing. This is the goal of becoming harmonized with the rest of the reality in such a way that the

148

thing and the reality complete itself so that the greatest amount of goodness is achieved.

One: Unity: Whole: These are the three individual goals of the fourth cause. The first goal tries to make the thing and the reality one. The second goal tries to form one identity or group identity with the reality. The third goal tries to achieve a harmony so that all the parts achieve a total wholeness. All things become one reality and contribute towards the oneness of the reality. All things become identified with the total reality; and all things work in a harmony in which the total goodness of the reality is realized.

FIRST CAUSE

ENTITY—The universal concept of becoming. That which is opposite to non-reality. It offers the first universal presentation of reality. On the other side of Entity is nothing.

POTENTIAL—It is the general idea offering the possibility of reality. This reality can be anything and anywhere but it offers a definite indication that something can become.

SUBSTRATE—This is the specified thing that is presented in a specified given reality. This offers a specified and determined becoming thing.

MATTER, FORM, MOTION—These are the three major material ingredients which bring about an individual becoming. Something individual is now presenting itself to a given reality. It is through these three material ingredients that the individual thing is allowed to present itself in a given reality. The matter determined which reality the thing will be presented. If a becoming thing has matter other than the matter of this reality the thing will present itself in another reality. The form specifies what the thing will become and the motion will individualize the thing.

SECOND CAUSE

BEING—The universal concept of development. This concept is the much confused bogy of the science of philosophy. It is the universal concept dealing with the formation and the development of the one thing which was presented through the first cause of becoming.

ACTUAL—This is the general concept of the thing which is to be developed in the second cause. It refers to something that is actually determined so that it may be fully developed. When something is actualized it is determined and now beginning the process of development of this actual thing.

SUBSTANCE—The specific thing to be developed in this reality is the thing called substance. This is the specified thing which will undergo the process of development of the actually presented one thing.

ESSENCE, EXISTENCE, OPERATION—These are the three principles through which the process of development will take place. Essence will develop the oneness of the being. Existence will develop the completeness of the being allowing the being to have a place in which to perform regular acts and to face the reality through a definite set of rules and regulations.

THIRD CAUSE

FRUITION—This is the universal idea of bringing forth products or fruits from the fully developed thing presented through the second cause.

IDEALIZATION—This is the general concept which is concerned with motivating the individual thing to bring forth some fruits from his singularity or individuality.

ILLUMINATION—This is the specific concept which is presented by the society to motivate the individual to bring forth some product from his self. It is that which the society specifies as desirable for producing by the individual members of the given society.

SINGULARITY, RELATIONSHIPS, FULNESS—These are the three values which the cause uses to allow fruition to take place in the individual. Singularity places the responsibility upon the individual by allowing the individual to recognize his uniqueness from all other individuals. Relationships allow the individual to be more effective in his fruitfulness and productiveness and this places the emphasis upon forming associations to allow more production to come forth. Fulness places the value of producing things as a personal achievement of the individual which allows the individual a measure of happiness for what he has brought forth.

FOURTH CAUSE

FINALIZATION—This is the universal goal of the thing which was first presented through the first cause. This is the universal concern of fitting the thing into the total world order seen and unseen.

REALIZED—This is the general concept which is concerned bringing about the full place for which the thing was introduced into the given reality.

SUBSTANTIAL—This is the specific concept which is concerned with bringing about the harmonization of the specified reality with the total reality in which it is concerned. This is the practicalization of the thing with its reality.

ONE, UNITY, WHOLE—These are the three individual goals which are presented to the individual thing so that a finalization can take place with the thing presented and with the reality in which it finds itself. The goal of oneness allows the thing to consider itself as a part of one reality or one society. The goal of unity allows the thing to become identified with the oneness of the reality. The thing and the reality can communicate with each other. The goal of wholeness allows the thing to consider itself as belonging to something in which without him the reality would lack its fullest presentation. The individual contributes his part to the wholeness of the reality.

EPILOGUE

The contents of this work is not considered as something original in the sense that no one has approached the subject before, just the opposite, for many have written and dealt with the subjects discussed in this work. What is considered to be originality is the framework in which the subjects are presented . . . through the four causes. Up to this work, all thinkers considered themselves presenting a view which was more true to reality than those who preceded them. It is the contention of this work that there are four basic views of reality and each view is based upon one of the four causes. To have a true picture of the total reality one must understand all the four causes and how they interrelate. Once the four causes are accepted as the framework in which to view reality, it is easily seen how the thinkers with their various views contribute to the overall picture of reality. Some will concentrate upon the first cause for that is usually the cause in which they are living. Others will bring out the second, third and fourth cause and each thinker will contribute something of value to the overall picture of reality.

With this in mind the bibliography that is presented contains the subject matter of all the four causes by various thinkers throughout history and by using the guide of the four causes one will be able to grasp the full picture of reality more so than without a framework in which to view things.

Works concerning the four causes can be divided into four areas: the universal view; the general view; the specific view; and the individualistic view.

In the universal view of reality we are concerned with the theories dealing with the creation of this reality which we experience and this is the view of the first cause from cosmology. In the universal view we would be concerned with the material development of this reality through the study of Astronomy. The intellectual theories as to the becoming of this reality would be dealt with in the field of Cosmology; and the religious belief of some creator necessary to bring about this becoming would be considered in the religious beliefs of mankind. Again we have the three basic ingredients of matter (astronomy); form (cosmology); and motion (religion).

The universal view concerning the second cause of reality would be that view with interests revolving around the development of this reality and of mankind. This is the view of the development of the species and the development of the societies of man.

The universal third view of reality would concern the fruition of the created reality. This view would concern itself with the products and the fruits that were produced by the creatures presented in this reality and in the total reality created and it also applies to the fruits produced by the creator. Thus this total reality can be considered as the fruition of the supreme creator.

The universal works concerning the fourth cause would deal with the realization of the total reality. These would concern themselves with the final purpose of all things and the final realization of all things. In the material realm the concern with the finalization would revolve around the one order and law with which all things are bound together in harmony. In the intellectual order the Chinese express this the best through their many views of the harmony that should prevail in all things. In the religious realm the finalization of this reality is expressed in the last judgment and the beautification of all things.

The general view of the four causes concern themselves with the science of archaeology, general historic development, the products of mankind and the completed realization of the societies of men.

The general view of the first cause is pre-history. Since the finding of Dr. L.S.B. Leakey in Olduvai Gorge south of Ethiopia and other similar findings it is generally agreed that the birthplace of man was in Africa. This is the material finding regarding the becoming of mankind. The intellectual understanding is best expressed by the Greeks and their views on the origin of life and early state of man can be found in the book by W.K.C. Guthrie IN THE BEGINNING (London 1957). The religious view concerning the general becoming naturally is found in the works of the BIBLE and other ancient religious beliefs held by people throughout the world.

The general view of the second cause would concern itself with the developments of the societies of mankind; the cultural or intellectual achievements of mankind; and the religious beliefs and development of mankind.

In this area all the works concerning the ancient development of societies such as the Egyptian, Ethiopian, Persian and the many other societies and civilizations which were developed during the formation of mankind. The culmination of this development was achieved by the Roman civilization which is the civilization from which almost all of the basic laws of mankind are derived.

In the general area of the formal development of mankind there naturally would be many books devoted to this subject because this is the area in which the intellectuals find their roots. The intellectual achievement and development of mankind was completed with the Greeks. Books such as William Chace Greene, THE ACHIEVEMENT OF GREECE (Cambridge 1923). The intellectual accomplishment can be found in WORKS OF ARISTOTLE, Edited by Richard McKeon (New York 1941) and THE DIALOGUES OF PLATO, Edited by B. Jowett (New York 1937). There are naturally a great number of works and commentaries of the works of the intellectual development of mankind and most of these concern the final achievement of the Greeks but generally all culture and intellectual development should belong in the general development of the second cause because the Greeks developed their ideas from those which were presented to them from older societies.

The general formal development of the religious belief of mankind was culminated through the Jewish religion in which the highest formation of religious beliefs was developed and formulated. Naturally the BIBLE is the chief source of this development but there are many beliefs held by people of the times that were similar to the Jews.

The general fruition of mankind is being achieved by the western civilization. This civilization in which we are a member is bringing forth all the products and all the fruits which mankind is capable of achieving. All the inventions and all the many products that have been produced in this world in such abundance have been the achievement of the western civilization. It is not books and works of the mind which are the overall achievement of western civilization but all the fruits and products which have been presented to mankind by this civilization. The intellectual development of western society is not the formation of systems of thought but the formation of schools in which the total majority of mankind could be instructed in one manner or another. The general religious achievement of western society has been the fruition and the spread of the Christian religion which as we have seen was the development and formation of the Jewish religion.

So generally speaking, the contribution to mankind of western society has been bringing forth the fruits and products which man is capable of producing. We in the western civilization are the workers of humanity.

The general realization of the fourth cause can be understood through the study of the Chinese civilization. This society places all the emphasis upon the purpose of reality. A few good works on this subject can be seen in Amury de Riencourt's THE SOUL OF CHINA (New York 1958) and a work edited by John K. Fairbanks, CHINESE THOUGHT AND INSTITUTIONS (Chicago 1957).

The specific working of the four causes can be understood in our society which we call western civilization. The first specific cause naturally refers to the becoming or the bringing to be of our society. This is the period of the migration of various tribes and clans to a definite place in which they settle and begin to become a definite society. This becoming is the period in which epic poetry is written. This is the period of the society in which if we had a Homer he would write our ILIAD and ODYSSEY. Instead of Homer we in the English world have our BEOWULF. This is the DARK AGES of our society but it is a period in which bringing to actuality is taking place . . . the period of becoming.

The specific formation of our civilization begins to take place around 1000 A.D. and this is the period in which the development of the being of the society will take place. Our schools and institutions of learning are developed in this period. The governments of the society are developed with the formation of a limited monarchy. The intellectual development of the church is accomplished through such works as Duns Scotus, Saint Bonaventure and Thomas Aquinas. See the BASIC WRITINGS OF SAINT THOMAS AQUINAS edited by Anton C. Pegis (New York, 1945). Since this was the time of the development of the society it was naturally the time of the being of the society and that is why there is so much work on the subject of being, such as Victor Michael Hamn PICO DELLA MIRANDOLA of BEING and UNITY (Wisconsin, 1943) ; Etienne Gilson BEING AND SOME PHILOSOPHERS (Toronto, 1949) ; C.R.S. Harris DUNS SCOTUS (New York, 1959).

We have in the second period of our civilization the development of a distinctive form of building called the Gothic construction; new social structures are developed in which the society is formed into one totality and is organized so that all the people of the society have a place and are allowed to perform some function in the society. This period is still represented in some parts of Europe with the emphasis upon the monarchy, upon the institutions of learning and upon the formal Catholic Church.

The specific working of the fruition of our society concerns the period which we call the modern age or the period of time in which we live. This period began about 1500 A.D. and it is concerned with the fruition of the society and the emphasis is upon the production of the individual. This period begins with the introduction of the new Christian church which places the emphasis upon the responsibility of the individual and this is the Protestant or the fruitional church. Naturally the three areas of any society will be affected by the new, so we have the three leading thinkers in the field of religion, thought and government represented by Jacques Maritain, THREE REFORMERS, Luther —Descartes—Rousseau (London, 1928); and we begin to recive some of the ideals presented by the utopian writers: Arthur E. Morgan, NOWHERE WAS SOMEWHERE: HOW HISTORY MAKES UTOPIAS AND HOW UTOPIAS MAKE HISTORY (Chapel Hill, 1946); Richard Gerber UTOPIAN FANTASY (London, 1955). We are now introduced to the third cause in our society with the emphasis upon the ideal and upon the fruition of the singular person. New governments are introduced with the rise of the autocrats who represent the rise of the great singular man and eventually the democratic government is introduced with the American experiment. The thinkers are now concerned with the problems of how the individual understands reality and this is to be seen in George Boas, DOMINANT THEMES OF MODERN PHILOSOPHY (New York, 1957) and in the works of Descartes, Albert G. A. Balz, DESCARTES AND THE MODERN MIND (New Haven, 1952). The idea of producing things and of bringing forth new things is exemplified in the idea of "progress," J. B. Bury, THE IDEA OF PROGRESS (London, 1921).

Now that we are leaving the third cause and entering the fourth cause in our civilization we will be considering more the oneness of the governments of the world and this is seen with the beginning of thinking towards one world government with the idea of the United Nations. We will be thinking in terms of Howard Munford Janes, ONE GREAT SOCIETY (New York, 1959) enabling all the people of the society to receive a good education. We will be thinking of the society in a way similar to Chester G. Starr, CIVILIZATION AND THE CAESARS (Ithaca, 1954) and we shall be thinking more of the Chinese thought and culture since they have concentrated upon the fourth cause during most of their history, see Arthur Waley, THREE WAYS OF THOUGHT IN ANCIENT CHINA (Garden City, 1939) and the books by Derk Bodde, CHINA'S FIRST UNIFIER, (Leiden, 1938) and Herrlee Glessner Creel, SINISM (Chicago, 1929).

We do not know what the future has in store for any person but we can say for certain that the emphasis will be upon the fourth cause which will place the achievement of the society upon the oneness of governments, the unity of all mankind and the wholeness of humanity.

The individual working of the causes in our society can be dated with the becoming of people from Europe into the new world. Since the United States represents the third cause more than any country of Europe and since the people who left the old world were those who for the most part were looking towards the new cause than just presenting itself to the society, we find in our individual society of the United States a slow migration of peoples coming to this new land. There were peoples of all kinds and descriptions but the people who were the main guiding lines for the formation of the new society were the Protestant or the fruitional Christian Church. These were the people who were to set the pace and the form of the society. From the coming of the Pilgrims in 1620 to the founding of the new society in the 1770s this was the period of becoming of this society. After the Declaration of Independence, the development of the new society took place and when the formation of the new society was threatened by the different views of bringing forth the fruit from the land there was a civil war to decide the issue. The South wanted to retain the second cause in the society which placed the emphasis upon the stable farm life and upon the development of the being of the society. The emphasis was upon nobility, intellectual learning and the formal church. The North placed emphasis upon the responsibility of each individual to produce from himself as much as possible with a dynamic economy, a government that did not interfere in the affairs of men and a religion which did not demand too much formal adherence to the rituals and dogmas of the Church.

After the Civil War decided the issue for the North the country went on with vigor to bring forth the fruits of the land, for that is the American Dream, the bringing forth of the third cause in society.

As the United States enters the fourth cause in its society a closer look at the Chinese view will be undertaken. With the means of transportation offered by the Western World there will be no bounds preventing the coming together of the third and the fourth cause. China built her wall to keep out the people from the north and from the Gobi regions but there is no wall preventing the western world from coming into more contact with the Chinese and this will be taking place in the near future. We can expect in the future a great number of books considering the oneness of mankind and the necessity of having one overall government ordering the material goods for the whole of mankind. We shall also have in the future the necessity for dialogue between all the peoples of the earth and this is a possibility with the methods of communication brought forth by Western technology. We shall also see the necessity of having the religious beliefs of mankind united under one complete body of religious aspiration for the whole mankind showing the working of the four causes. The Southern view expressed the becoming of things and this is the view from the Father. The Northern view expressing the formation or the development of the Being of mankind is the view expressing the second person of the Supreme

Trinity, the Son. The third view expressed by the western civilization expressed the working of the Spirit which brings forth the fruits from the beings. Finally the fourth view expressed by the Eastern Society, stressing the oneness, unity and goodness of all reality.